the lamp

To Dawn

the lamp

Be Aglow and Burning with the Spirit

Sandra Strange

SANDRA STRANGE

The Lamp, Be Aglow and Burning with the Spirit
Copyright © 2015 Sandra Strange

Available from Amazon.com, CreateSpace.com, and other retail outlets

ISBN-13: 978-1511524957
ISBN-10: 1511524952

This book is dedicated with love to my daughters
Susan Worley Ekhoff and Sandy Worley Thompson.
You are the joy of my life.

Honor your father and your mother,
that your days may be long upon the land
which the Lord your God is giving you.
Ex. 20:12

I am honored by you.

S.S.

Table of Contents

My Family – God's Gift
Introduction

Dear Reader
My Prayer

Acknowledgments

My daughter Susan has encouraged me to write my story for many years. Her passion for preserving family history and conviction that God's beautiful work in our lives *must* be recorded for His glory stoked my call to write. As my content editor she brought out the deeper me and unveiled the details of my testimony. She also formatted the book. Thank you. We did it!

Deepest thanks to Mary Royster, my friend of nearly forty years. The Holy Spirit gave Mary the revelation that exploded within me – *now* is God's time to write your book! Then she offered to type and help edit it, patiently working beside me for a year and a half. I am forever indebted to you.

My heartfelt thanks to Elizabeth Oaks and Lydia Ekhoff for their additional edits.

Without each of these participants in the process, this book would not be what it has become.

As you read the stories that follow, it will be evident that the Lord has used many people to teach me His ways. These inner circle women have stood by me through it all, over many years:

- *My Aglow leadership friends:* Rita Dupont, Penny Lee, Janice Newcomb, Mary Royster, and Anna Laura Simpson;
- *My Emmaus reunion group:* Nancy Batterman, Kathy Connor, Linda Jarosz, Martha Mitchell, Peg Purgason, and Martha Sue Thompson;
- *My First Presbyterian friends:* Pat Argyrakis, Gwen Baucom, Gerry Belton, Pat Bolt, Susie Crews, Bernadine Hayes, Ina Ingram, Elaine Lea, Lee Norman, Mary Ann Shelton, and Nancy Wilson.

You are each an inspiration and I love you.

About the Cover

The cover was jointly designed by my daughter Susan and granddaughter Hannah. Susan is a graduate of Oral Roberts University with a degree in commercial art and Hannah is a graduate of Moody Bible Institute with a degree in counseling.

Their model is Annie Hogle. Annie is sixteen years old, the third of six children and home schooled. She loves basketball and homemaking. Annie is eager to please and has a servant's heart.

The ceramic lamp is from Jerusalem, a gift from Hannah, purchased for the book's graphic design.

My Family – God's Gift

Parents –

Mary Anna Martin and George Lanier Easley

Siblings –

Mary Franklin, Patricia Mosher, Dorothy Van Auken, George Easley, and James Easley

Marriages –

Sandra Bagby Easley and Billy Anderson Worley, January 16, 1960
Sandra Easley Worley and Rice Gwynn Strange, June 3, 1978

Children, Grandchildren, Great-grandchildren –

Susan Worley and Richard Ekhoff –
Benjamin Ekhoff, Hannah and David George and their daughter Eleanor; Lydia, Mary, Samuel, Julia, and John Ekhoff

Sandy Worley and Rodney Thompson –
David, Jr. and Liz Hoskins and their son Graham; Rebekah and Anthony Formigoni and their daughter Emmah; Allison and Christian Barraza and their children: Gabriel, Danny, Evelyn, and Lillian; Rachel, Sarah, and Daniel Hoskins; Brad and Ryan Thompson

Sandra Easley Worley and Rice Gwynn Strange –
Rice's children: Ann and Steve Jurcezk and their daughters, Kimberly and Sarah; Rice, Jr. and Nathalie Strange and their son Brent

Introduction

Shortly before midnight on New Year's Eve 1966, I did a heartrending year in review. In January my father-in-law had had a massive heart attack and died while shoveling snow. After his father's death my husband Bill Worley simply gave up. He had been struggling with alcoholism for years and now the addiction spiraled out of control. All he did was work, sleep, and drink, as our marriage and finances deteriorated.

I was a twenty-nine year-old registered nurse married to an alcoholic, practically raising our two small daughters alone. In my desperation I had spent the past year searching for meaning for my life. I read my horoscope, visited a fortuneteller, played with a Ouija board, and even became interested in witchcraft. I had also considered calling the Catholic priest in town to see what was involved in becoming Catholic. I was attracted to the mystery of the Mass, and all the Catholics I knew seemed to have more going for them than I did.

On that fateful New Year's Eve, feeling lost and alone - no one to even cry with - I pulled out the 1966 calendar and wrote in large letters, "This has been the worst year of my life!" I had always loved New Year's Eve. It represented a chance to make a happy new start. But I couldn't even muster *hope* for the New Year, much less *happiness.*

In these quiet moments of reflection, a wrenching question demanded my attention: Should I keep plodding - go to work, go to church, and love my family as best I could - or should I just give up? The clock struck midnight; 1967 had arrived.

These are stories of my spiritual journey from 1966 - 2015. It is my legacy to my daughters, grandchildren, and great-grandchildren, stories of love, life, and light.

For You are my lamp, O Lord;
The Lord shall enlighten my darkness.
For by You I can run against a troop;
By my God I can leap over a wall.

II Samuel 22:29-30

part one
stories *of* love

LOVE is the high esteem

that God has

for His human children

and the high regard

which they in turn should have

for Him and other people.

Nelson's Illustrated Bible Dictionary[1]

Take Time to Be Holy

January settled in, bitter cold with frequent snows. I was working the graveyard shift at the hospital as an R.N. Duties complete, I clocked out on this particular Sunday morning wondering how I would make it through another day. But there was no time to think about me.

Arriving home, Susan, age six, and Sandy, age three, greeted me with hugs and happy chatter, ready for breakfast. I automatically dressed my daughters and myself for the 8:30 a.m. service and left for church. My husband Bill never went with us, not even on Easter or Christmas.

I moved to my usual pew in the right front portion of the sanctuary and sank listlessly into my seat. In the ensuing quiet I evaluated my situation. Our income had been insufficient for our bills for some time. It had been one year since the death of Bill's dad – I wondered if he had been sober since. And I had spent the last year on a destructive course of my own, searching for meaning for my life.

Despite my exhaustion and distraction, the sermon caught my attention from the start. I listened intently as the minister preached on *holiness* from I Peter 1:15-16. He explained that holiness is one of the essential elements of God's nature and He requires it of His children. God is holy and we are to be holy, which is our righteousness. Thankfully, he concluded with a practical plan to discover the components of holiness:

- Set aside a place and time to meet with God for fifteen minutes each day.
- Sing or read through a hymn.
- Read a portion of the Bible.
- Pray. He talked of prayer as a conversation with a friend. He encouraged us to pour out all our troubles to our Father in Heaven and then spend time listening. He explained that God speaks in different ways, but we would learn to recognize His voice as we spent time with Him.

As I absorbed this message, I was consumed by the desire for holiness. I remember thinking that if I could choose between holiness and anything else – even a large amount of money or Bill's freedom from alcoholism – I would choose holiness. I was excited. Here was something I could do!

I started my quest the very next morning. I picked our bedroom for my specific place and 10 a.m. as my appointed time, then completed all the steps faithfully every day. How could I know I was being prepared for a personal encounter with my God?

At the end of April, my hometown Danville, Virginia, publicized a citywide revival. Churches of different denominations from all over town were cosponsoring this event. My mother-in-law called on Sunday afternoon to see if we were going to the opening night. I didn't know much about it, since my church was not participating, but I had a long list of mental excuses for refusing. Without explanation I countered, "No, we're not going." She encouraged that the services would continue all week. Perhaps we could go another night.

2

Monday morning I opened the newspaper to a huge article on the revival with a picture that covered both sides of the first spread. As I was reading, Bill came up behind me. After studying the picture and article, he questioned, "Do you want to go?" I was thrilled at the thought of going, but answered simply and evenly, "Yes, let's go."

That evening Bill's sister Mary Abbott kept our girls while we went to the revival. It was the first time I had ever been to anything like it. The crowd had been estimated at 1,000 the night before, and Neal's Warehouse was packed again for the second night. The singing was heartfelt, the prayers earnest and meaningful, the sermon interesting. When it was over, I didn't want to leave.

The next day Bill said he didn't want to go back, but he was happy for me to go. I didn't hesitate. Off I went every night without a backward glance.

On Wednesday evening the evangelist gave his testimony. He had been an alcoholic and God had healed him. I sat there in shocked wonder. I didn't know God could heal anyone from anything, much less alcoholism. His written testimony was for sale, so I bought it, took it home, and read it before going to bed.

The next morning I told Bill about the testimony and the book. He did read the book but made no comment.

As the week progressed and I gathered spiritual steam, I came to a strong realization – Bill needed to be saved! So I thought up a plan to move him in that direction. On Saturday night I would somehow convince Bill to go back to the revival with me and when the invitation was given, I would go to the altar and rededicate my life. I believed if I did that, he would follow and be saved.

Saturday came. My mother-in-law was pleased with my plan and agreed to baby-sit for us. And to my surprise Bill agreed to go. As an extra bonus, Bill's sister Mary was going with us. Piling into the front seat, laughing and talking, we lit up our cigarettes and headed to the service.

I have no idea what the sermon was about that night – I was waiting for the altar call. As soon as it was given, I jumped up and was the first to reach the front of the room. I stopped before the platform and bowed my head. As I stood there, wondering how to rededicate my life, I was confronted with the person of Jesus Christ. My eyes were closed, but I somehow knew Jesus was standing in front of me. I heard Him say, "You are a sinner." That was a shock! I was a faithful church member after all. I had always thought of myself as a good person. But standing transparently before Him, my whole life exposed to His gaze, I knew He was right. Thankfully, I had learned that week how to confess sins. Immediately, I did that and then asked Him to save me. At once I was bathed in warm love from the top of my head to the soles of my feet. I was washed and washed.

When this wonderful cleansing experience ended, I knew my sins were gone and I was white as snow. I was bursting with love, peace, and joy. To my mind came the words, *"They went jumping and leaping and praising the Lord!" (Acts 3:8)* At that time I didn't know those words were in the Bible. But of course, it was an unacceptable thing to do, so I constrained myself.

When I looked around, I was startled to see so many people at the altar – and Bill was standing behind me!

After the service those who had responded to the altar call were escorted to another room for personal counseling. We were asked a series of questions to clarify our decision. I readily proclaimed that I was a sinner and knew Jesus had saved me. Bill too confessed that he knew he was a sinner, but he could not believe that God was personal or cared anything about him. During the forty-five minute discussion that followed, the persistent counselors assigned to him could not convince him otherwise.

Back in the car Bill and Mary lit up their cigarettes, but I had no desire for one.

As we entered the house together fifteen minutes later, I joyfully announced, "I'm born again!" (John 3) Bill's mother didn't even try to mask her frustration that it was I – not Bill – who had been saved. The plan had certainly unfolded outside our predetermined plan. But I was so changed and filled with God's Spirit her disappointment didn't hurt me. Blissfully, expectantly, I began my new life in Jesus. It was May 6, 1967.

I have learned the importance of pursuing a relationship with the Lord by spending time with Him daily, reading my Bible, praising Him in song, and conversing with Him through prayer. But these disciplines do not make us holy; they add substance to our search for holiness. Only Jesus' death on the cross makes us holy.

When I met Jesus at the altar during the revival I experienced the One who is Holy and entered into Him. After that encounter the Holy Spirit in me continued to teach me about a life of holiness as I obeyed His Word.

Jesus is an extremely personal God. He loves us so much.

But as He who called you is holy,
you also be holy in all your conduct.
Because it is written,
"Be holy for I am holy."
I Peter 1:15-16

Not Die, but Live

Only a week later, I was tested in my new faith . . .

It all started on a gorgeous Sunday morning, Mother's Day. I felt truly honored as a wife and a mother that day. It had been a long time since I had felt good about *me*. Bill was at church with us – I knew this was a miracle. Best of all my heart was overflowing with the love of God. Spring was in full bloom and so was I.

One of the congregational hymns that morning was "O For A Thousand Tongues To Sing." As I joined in with an awakened spirit, I realized that I had heard this hymn many times during my years of church attendance, but I had never understood it. Now I thought, "This is what I need – 'a thousand tongues' to tell of my Savior and His love." Suddenly, I couldn't sing or hear the others singing. I seemed to be immersed in a solemn quiet where I clearly heard the voice of Jesus say, "I gave My life for you; will you give your life for Me?"

"Yes, I will give my life for You."

At my affirmative something that felt like depression settled in. I reasoned that if Jesus wanted my life, I must be about to die. My mind digressing, I thought of all the possible ways it could happen. I looked at my husband and daughters and thought my heart would break.

At that time I didn't know about our enemy satan and how he could torment us by putting thoughts into our minds. I was on a big adventure, receiving the love of Jesus, becoming a new person, and experiencing the enemy all at the same time.

After church we went to my mother-in-law's home for lunch and our Mother's Day celebration. Numb with fear and loss, I barely did what was required of me. The hope that cheered me through the visit was that we were going to my parents' home for the afternoon. They lived eighteen miles away in Chatham, Virginia. I knew that as soon as I saw my mother, I would be all right. She was my uncontested rock.

When we arrived at my parents' home and were almost to the porch, I remembered her gift in the car. The family went on into house while I returned to the car to retrieve it. I had hurried back up the walk and had my hand on the doorknob when the Lord spoke for the second time that day. "Choose. Choose between Me and your mother." I discerned that every dependence I had placed in my mother must now be transferred to Jesus. Determined to do what I knew was right, I whispered in my heart, "I choose You, Lord." Thundering through my mind came the words, *"The Lord your God is a jealous God" (Deuteronomy 4:24).* This relinquishment was the final blow. When I entered the house and handed Mother our gift, I burst into tears. We finally had to leave because I couldn't stop crying.

In the isolation of the car I calmed myself, but when I tried to tell Bill what had happened, the tears started again. Finally he comforted, "Maybe you need to live this for awhile before you try to talk about it." It was wise advice, so we talked of other things the rest of the way home.

But by the next morning I was desperate: I needed counsel. My new friend and neighbor Joanne Dehaven was the only person I could think of who might possibly help me. She was a pastor's wife and I thought she would certainly know more about God than me. Hope rising, I hurried around the block to her home. Seeing my obvious distress, she welcomed me to sit down with her on the pleasant front porch where we could have privacy. Gratefully, I poured out all that had happened the day before and she prayed with me.

Over the next week Joanne shared her insights. She began by telling me about our enemy and how he was trying to steal the freedom God had given me, that Jesus had my heart, but satan was still battling for my mind. Then she read James 4:7–8 to me: *"Therefore submit to God. Resist the devil (satan) and he will flee from you. Draw near to God and He will draw near to you."* I didn't believe in satan or hell, so I didn't know what to think.

She also gave me a list of scriptures to read and I often meditated on them. The dark depression still pressed in and I believed I wouldn't live much longer, but I studied and stood against the enemy as best I could using the Word of God.

Joanne continued to be a supportive friend and came to our home several evenings. Bill became interested in these sessions and joined us, listening to my questions about the Christian life. He sometimes injected questions of his own. I don't remember the exact questions we asked or the answers Joanne gave us; I just remember her patience, and how we tried to apply her answers to our lives. She suggested that Bill read the Gospel of John, explaining that it revealed Jesus. Bill took her advice and read it.

One summer morning a few months later, I was standing at the kitchen sink washing dishes when I suddenly realized that the darkness was gone – absolutely gone. Thinking back, I marveled anew at all that had happened to Bill and me in so short a time.

Then Jesus spoke to me clarifying, "Not *die,* but *live* for Me." Dishcloth in hand, a hymn of response came to mind and I sang it aloud to Him as a love song.

> Living for Jesus, a life that is true,
> Striving to please You in all that I do,
> Yielding allegiance, glad-hearted and free,
> This is the pathway of blessing for me.
>
> O Jesus, Lord and Savior, I give myself to You
> For You, in Your atonement, did give Yourself for me;

I own no other Master, my heart shall be Your throne
My life I give, henceforth to live, O Christ, for You alone.[2]

As I continued spending time in the Word each day, I found Psalm 118:17, and it became the cry of my heart: *"I will not die but live and declare the works of the Lord."*

———————————

During this time of rapid growth, I learned that I died with Jesus and He had come to live in me. In my new life it was imperative that I transfer my dependence from my mother to Jesus. And it was a good thing I did – just three months later we moved to Atlanta and I couldn't depend on her presence to give me strength.

I have also learned that there is both a natural life and spiritual life. We may not believe that Jesus is the Son of God, and we may not believe in the existence of satan; never the less, we are all influenced by the one true God with His angels and by satan and his demons. A war is continuously raging for our mind, will, and emotions.

Bill's Fleece

On this hot Friday morning in mid-July, I was increasingly aware that my daily time for Bible reading was slipping past. Our family had been invited to visit friends in the Shenandoah Valley of Virginia. In the midst of the busy preparations all I wanted to do was read my Bible. I was so drawn to it that I would iron for a bit, sit down and try to read, then jump up to check on the girls in the back yard. On and on it went until around about 10:30 a.m.

Then the phone rang; my neighbor across the street was calling to invite my girls to play with her children and have lunch. What a surprise! She had never offered a play date before. After walking the girls across the street, I decisively set the ironing aside, sat down at the kitchen table, and opened my Bible.

Around noon I reached the last chapter of I Thessalonians. Suddenly, the words seemed to sparkle and jump right off the page. I blinked, focused, and reread these words: *"Rejoice always, pray without ceasing, in everything give thanks; for this is the will of the Father in Christ Jesus for you"* *(I Thessalonians 5:16-18)*. Somehow I knew something was going to happen that I would think was terrible, but I was to praise and thank God anyway. I determined to obey this instruction, wondering what the "something" would be and closed my Bible. All the while I was encompassed with peace. In a surprisingly short time, my preparations for the weekend were complete.

Around 4:00 o'clock a friend dropped by with a book she thought would bless me in my new walk with Christ: *Beyond Ourselves*[3] by Catherine Marshall. I wanted to start reading right away, but the insistent ringing of the phone sidetracked me.

It was Bill's employer with bad news. He had just fired Bill, but he wasn't sure he understood that. Bill had been sitting at his desk all day without moving. With genuine compassion he expressed his concern that drugs may be an issue and encouraged me to get help. Stunned, I hung up the phone – and as I did I knew at once that this was the event for which I had been prepared. Pushing away panic, I thanked my Father in Heaven and determined to trust Him to take care of us.

Thirty minutes later Bill walked into the house. He was staring straight ahead like a zombie. As soon as I saw him, I realized what had happened. Several weeks earlier he had been determined to stop drinking and had gone to a physician for help. He was given a prescription for Valium and obviously had started drinking again while taking it. How he arrived safely, I'll never know. He passed me without speaking and went upstairs, where he collapsed across our bed.

I waited a little while before going up to check on him so I could emotionally prepare myself. I had discovered that summer that there is a fine line between love and hate. Slipping upstairs, I wondered which emotion I would experience this time. But when I stood before the bed, I was uncharacteristically overcome with compassion and loved him exactly the way he was. This anointing in the love of God changed me and my relationship with Bill. All the cumulative negative emotions of seven years of marriage were healed in a single moment.

My next thought was to call Bill's sister Mary and ask her to help me waken him. But no matter what we tried, we couldn't rouse him. As a nurse, I knew this was not a medical emergency. There was nothing to do but let him sleep.

Mary stayed while I finished my trip preparations then together we studied the Virginia map and marked the route to the Shenandoah Valley. I had driven to my parent's home thirty minutes away, but had never read a road map, so I truly appreciated her help.

Mary offered to return the next morning to see us off and was back early as promised. The effect of the Valium/alcohol combination was wearing off. We were able to get Bill dressed and downstairs where we all had coffee together. After breakfast Mary and I packed the car and helped Bill into the backseat where he promptly went back to sleep.

We began our trip with the girls on the front seat beside me, excited to be going to see their friends. It was a dreary morning in pouring rain. I marvel as I write this that it never occurred to me not to go. This was my life, and I had learned to cope with the daily frustrations of it.

Bill woke at some point and we stopped for lunch. After eating he was alert and back to the person I knew and loved. We talked very little about yesterday's events as the girls were with us, but I told him about his job – he didn't know he had been fired and thought he had worked all day. As we continued the journey the sun peeked out and my spirit brightened. We were soon at the home of our friends.

This visit was a gift from God. The family had a lovely home on the Shenandoah River with inviting lawn chairs on the bank. The river was shallow enough for the children to splash all afternoon. Bill was in his element, wading in the river, playing games with the children, and sitting on the front porch enjoying the magnificent view of the mountains, as we visited with our friends.

Saturday evening I finally had a chance to open *Beyond Ourselves*. It seemed that the author had answered every question I had ever heard Bill ask about God in the opening paragraphs of chapter one. Closing the book, I joined him on the front porch. "Just read the first chapter," I encouraged.

Bill stayed up most of the night pouring over the pages and had finished the book by the time we left Sunday afternoon. Some things the author had written had really impacted him, and he read those passages to me as we traveled home. I listened in wonder, sharing his interest, glimpsing a life of fellowship with each other and the Lord we didn't know existed. The children were asleep in the backseat, so we were able to talk about our situation: Neither of us was employed. I could easily find a nursing position, but was that the right thing to do? Bill was still an alcoholic. We were at a major crossroads. Which way should we go?

As we talked, an idea occurred to me. "Bill, what if we take two weeks without looking for jobs. Let's pray and ask God to show us His will." Bill was skeptical; he had no conviction that God could or would do anything about his most pressing problem – alcoholism, but he agreed to this plan. We decided to pray alone and together and wait in faith for God to show us our next step.

God's beautiful plan began to unfold just hours later. On Monday morning, Bill stepped into the kitchen doorway and asked, "Do you see anything different about me?" I looked carefully, but didn't see a thing. Then he pointed to his right eye. (For months he had endured a small white cyst in the lower left corner of his eye. He was conscious of it all the time. He had been to a surgeon, who told him it was too deep and too close to his eye to be removed.)

Bill shouted, "It's gone!" Sure enough, the cyst was gone. Then he shared that Saturday night he had looked into the mirror and cried out to God, "If You are real and care anything about me, take this cyst away." God had performed a miracle and Bill knew without question that he had encountered his very personal, powerful God.

Monday night he privately whispered his most desperate prayer. "Take away my desire to drink."

On Wednesday morning a similar scene was repeated. That husband of mine stood in the kitchen doorway and asked, "Do you see anything different about me?" Somehow it struck me as funny, so smiling hugely I looked, but didn't see anything

13

different. In an awed voice he announced, "I awakened this morning and didn't want a drink and knew I never would again."

I asked him why he thought I could see something different. He said, "After the revival I saw something different in you and I wanted you to see something different in me." This was day three.

On day four, Bill knelt at his father's grave and gave Jesus his life.

At the end of the two specified weeks, Bill decided he wanted to learn more about his newfound Savior and Healer. He thought the best way to pursue this goal was to attend seminary, so he submitted applications to Duke University in Durham, North Carolina, as well as Emory University in Atlanta, Georgia.

By the end of August he had been accepted at Candler School of Theology, Emory University, and our house was for sale. We would be moving to Atlanta in a little over a week. We had one weekend to find a place to live, a nursing position for me, and a school for Susan, who was starting first grade. We decided to make a quick scouting trip to Atlanta.

When we arrived on campus, I went straight to the Emory University Hospital, filled out an application, was interviewed and hired.

Meanwhile Bill went to the university housing department and applied for a two-bedroom apartment. We were fifty-fourth on the list. The rest of the day was spent apartment hunting, but all the apartments we visited were either too expensive or too far away from campus – we had only one car.

On our way out of town we stopped again by the housing department. Bill went in to tell them we had been unsuccessful in our search and to ask them to let us know if anything became available. In just a few minutes he rushed out of the building with a key in his hand. There had been a meeting that day, and out of fifty-four applicants, we had been deemed the most needy for the very last vacant apartment.

Completely overwhelmed and with thanksgiving in our hearts, we went straight to our apartment, home for the next four years. The downstairs had a combined living and dining area with a tiny kitchen. Upstairs were two bedrooms and a bath. We thought it was magnificent – and as a bonus, the school bus for the local elementary school stopped right in front of our apartment complex.

During this weekend my mind went back to my Mother's Day experience when Jesus had required that I *choose*. He was rightfully the center of my life and was proving Himself sufficient for me.

We headed back to Danville in silent awe. This day of the Lord's miraculous provision came as a "wrapped gift" on my thirtieth birthday, September 1, 1967.

I have learned conclusively that nothing is too hard for our enormous God. We serve a God of miracles. He heals broken people and changes difficult circumstances in ways we cannot fathom. His presence is our peace. Joyful, joyful, we adore You!

You are to Tithe

In the week following our Atlanta scouting trip, we packed and prepared to move with joy, but we were concerned that our house had still not sold. The only showing had been in early August.

I still remember that specific day. The realtor called to say he was bringing someone by in about an hour. In the interim between the call and their arrival, the Holy Spirit clearly spoke in my heart, "You are to tithe." I knew He had spoken and I knew what that meant. But how could we possibly obey? A tithe would be ten percent of our income. I hadn't worked all summer and Bill had been fired from his job in July. We had fifty dollars in the bank. Ten percent of fifty dollars was five dollars – a huge amount of money in 1967. We could buy a couple of bags of groceries with five dollars.

When Bill came home for lunch, I relayed what the Lord had said. After thinking for a while, he mused, "I don't see how we can do it, but God spoke to *you*. Do what you think is best." I debated in my mind into the afternoon, but after weighing our immediate needs (groceries, gas to travel to Atlanta, and a U-

Haul rental fee) with the reality of our checking account balance, I dismissed the idea of tithing.

The first weekend in September, we transitioned to a new life in Atlanta. Our house had not sold and we had to borrow $1,000 to move. Thankfully, I had a nursing job waiting for me and went right to work, and the G-I Bill funded Bill's tuition and books. But with one income, the Danville house payment, apartment rent, and our monthly expenses, we lived hand-to-mouth. We tried not to worry, trusting God for everything. Months passed into a year and still the house did not sell.

Spring, a year and a half later, we went back to Danville for a four-day Easter holiday. We always enjoyed these trips home. This visit we were particular threadbare and weary.

The weekend was all we had hoped for. The Virginia spring was bright with azalea, dogwood and redbud blooms, the glory of Easter all around us. We attended my parent's church on Easter morning and stayed for lunch. Later we had dinner with Bill's family.

Aware of our tight budget, our families typically loaded us up with canned goods, tins of goodies, and cash as we set out for Atlanta, but this time, no one gave us anything.

Back in Atlanta on Monday evening the stark reality of our situation set in. Inspecting our cupboard, I found we had enough food – if we stretched it - for three to four days. We had five dollars in cash designated for Susan's school lunch ticket, and one or two gallons of gas in the car. Payday was a distant ten days away.

I was working second shift that month, so I was home when the mail arrived Tuesday morning. Amidst the various bills was our church's annual pledge letter. A tithing card and brochure were included.

That brochure made a lifelong impression that I committed to heart and soul. The illustration was in cartoon format and the narrative read as follows: God gave a man ten apples. The man was to use three apples for food, three for shelter, and three for clothing. He was to give one back to God to thank Him for the other nine. The man used three apples for

17

food, three for shelter, and three for clothing. The tenth apple seemed bigger and redder than the other nine, so the man ate the apple and gave the core to God.

I was stricken. God had not said to me, "Do you want to tithe?" He had said, "You *are* to tithe." This time I didn't even wonder how we would do it. I determined to obey. I placed the letter, tithe card, and brochure on Bill's desk with a note stating, "We are to tithe!" and left for work.

By the time I arrived home that night, Bill had calculated our tithe from my gross income, and had placed the appropriate amount on the pledge card along with his signature. With conviction and joy I placed my name below his, sealed the card in an envelope, and sent it back to our church with Wednesday's mail. We were now committed.

On Thursday morning we received a surprise check for twenty-five dollars from one of our pastors with a personal note saying he remembered the financial strain of seminary. Here miraculously was our food and gas provision. How we praised and thanked God!

By Wednesday of the next week, our house in Danville had sold. If this were not enough of a confirmation of God's faithfulness, an anonymous friend sent us a gift of $150.00 that very same week. Tithing was established as our spiritual habit from that time on. After all these years I can testify that the Lord has more than provided for all my financial needs.

I learned two important life lessons – the hard way:

- When God speaks, we must promptly obey.
- In the light of all God has done for us, tithing, giving offerings, and blessing others is the only way of life for His people.

"For I am the Lord, I do not change;
Therefore you are not consumed, O sons of Jacob.
Yet from the days of your fathers
You have gone away from My ordinances

And have not kept them.
Return to Me, and I will return to you,"
Says the Lord of hosts.
"But you said,
'In what way shall we return?'
"Will a man rob God?
Yet you have robbed Me!
But you say,
'In what way have we robbed You?'
In tithes and offerings.
You are cursed with a curse,
For you have robbed Me,
Even this whole nation.
Bring all the tithes into the storehouse,
That there may be food in My house,
And try Me now in this,"
Says the Lord of hosts,
"If I will not open for you the windows of heaven
And pour out for you such blessing
That there will not be room enough to receive it.

Malachi 3:6 – 10

Set Your House in Order

When we arrived in Atlanta the Charismatic Movement was in full swing, a hub of spiritual revival, and we were drawn into the midst of it. The focus of this move of God was the works of the Holy Spirit. New friends included us in prayer groups, Bible studies, and retreats. We attended meetings where keynote speakers like Derek Prince taught about life in the Spirit. We went to healing services, heard fresh teachings from the book of Acts and many personal testimonies. Our spiritual lives grew exponentially.

One night while at a prayer meeting in the home of friends, hands were laid on us to receive the baptism of the Holy Spirit, an experience where we invited the Holy Spirit to come in His fullness and launch us into a deeper relationship with Him.

In addition our family joined University Heights United Methodist Church and became active in the ministries there. Reverend Sanders, our minister, visited our home frequently. This friendship encouraged Bill.

And so four wonderful years passed (1967 – 71): years of accelerated spiritual growth, deepening family relationships, and establishing new friendships.

When Bill graduated from seminary in May of 1971, he had no clear direction for ministry. Since he was no longer a student at Emory, we moved from university housing to a new apartment in Decatur, GA as we continued to consider our options. Bill didn't have a strong call to preach, but thought serving a church would be a good beginning, so he planned to contact the Virginia Conference of the United Methodist Church at the first of the year.

Early in January our lives unexpectedly changed course. It all began just before dinner one night as Bill took a quick shower. I was finishing the dinner preparations when he called to me from the bathroom. Pale and in obvious pain, he explained that as he switched off the hot water for a cold splash he had experienced a sudden, severe pain in his left arm.

Dinner forgotten, we hurried to the emergency room. Hours later, we learned he had a blood clot in his arm, and he was admitted to the hospital for treatment and further testing.

The next morning his doctor pulled me aside for a consultation on Bill's condition. A severe infection had been discovered in two valves of his heart, a condition called endocarditis (endō kär'dītis). When I questioned him about how this could have happened, his doctor shared the probable cause: Bill had reported having a tooth pulled several weeks before. The infection was probably released into his blood stream at that time, settling in his heart valves. He prescribed a hospital stay of up to four weeks with daily IV antibiotic infusions. The doctor was vague about complete recovery, "It will depend on the effectiveness of the antibiotics. We should know in a month." As he spoke, perspiration was literally dripping off the ends of my fingertips and my heart was crying out to God, "Please help us!"

Thankfully, I was working first shift and was exempt from weekend duty while Bill was hospitalized. Our lives were re-centered around his hospital room. I packed a sandwich and spent my lunch break with him. Every evening after an early dinner, the girls and I went to the hospital and stayed until the end of visiting hours was announced over the intercom system. On weekends we camped out at the hospital. Susan and Sandy shared school events and their dad played games with them. The girl's weekend treat was lunch in the hospital cafeteria.

January 16 was our twelfth wedding anniversary. We planned a big celebration for the following year when everything would certainly be back to normal.

Every night I prayed that the phone would not ring until morning and continued my intense prayers for his healing.

A few days before his discharge date, I slipped to Bill's room for our usual lunchtime visit. I had no sooner passed the threshold when Bill began to share: "During the night I awakened and thought I was dying." While I tried to grasp this news, he hurried on, "I grabbed my Bible and it fell open to this book and my eyes fell on this verse." Handing me his Bible with the indicated verse already underlined, he added, "I'm not going to get well."

Taking the Bible, I read the verse for myself, *"Thus says the Lord: "Set your house in order for you shall die, and not live" (II Kings 20:1b).* Hardly breathing, I read the rest of the chapter. It was the story of King Hezekiah, who was sick and near death. When The Lord sent the prophet Isaiah to confirm that he would not live, Hezekiah humbly prayed, and God granted him an additional fifteen years of life.

Bill was convinced that God had spoken definitively, but I could not – *I would not* – accept the prophecy. I skipped down to the fifteen-year extension, held on with both hands, and refused to even discuss to it with him.

Bill was discharged from the hospital in early February. His doctor was still unsure about a complete healing of the infection, but prescribed oral antibiotics and encouraged him to be as active as he could.

On Bill's first weekend home, his mother, sister and brother-in-law Mary and Raymond visited for a long weekend. The children were ecstatic; their visit cheered us all. And then on February 22, we celebrated Bill's fortieth birthday. The girls made cards and decorations and I made a special dinner.

But in the midst of these celebrations, Bill steadily "set his house in order." He showed me where the receipts for our taxes were kept and told me where to file them. He showed me where our important papers were boxed and encouraged me to build a house. I listened without comment. I still couldn't accept that he was dying; I refused to even think about it. When I suggested that we go to Danville for Easter, he looked at me sadly. "Please, don't wish my time away," he said.

In late February, I arrived home from work, to find Bill looking particularly pale and tired. I pushed down the alarm I felt, and listened as he related walking the girls the short half-mile to school that morning. At about the halfway point he had become so breathless and weak he thought he was going to die right there. He had sent the children on to school with the assurance he would be fine, but had to sit on a wall for thirty minutes before he was able to walk home.

On March 7th as I was readying for bed, Bill called from the study, "Should I finish this tonight, or wait until morning?" Since graduation from seminary, Bill had taken up a hobby of converting illustrations from Joan Walsh Anglund's children's books to 8 by 10" pen and ink drawings which he framed for our home. I came into the room and looked over his shoulder at a beautiful pencil drawing of a little girl peering around the trunk of a large tree. It was about half inked. Glancing at Bill I replied, "Wait until morning. You look tired." He took my advice and we headed to bed.

As the Lord would have it, March 8th was my day off. After Susan and Sandy left for school, I went to our bedroom to ask if Bill was ready for breakfast. Coming out of the bathroom he replied, "No, I think I'll sack out a little while longer." I smiled and nodded. I needed to pay bills, go to the post office, and get my hair cut. When I returned, we could have lunch together.

Bill went back to bed and I went to the kitchen table to write the checks. I was almost finished when I heard loud snoring coming from our bedroom. Looking up, I listened intently for a moment. It stopped then started again. Something about the sound seemed unusual. Concerned, but not unduly alarmed, I headed down the hall to check on him. As I entered our bedroom he took his last breath.

I picked up the bedroom phone five times and couldn't think of "zero for operator." (There was no 911 service at that time.) Running next door, I banged with both fists on my neighbor's door until her angry face appeared. After a hurried explanation she graciously called for an ambulance and waited for them to arrive, while I raced back to Bill and started mouth-to-mouth resuscitation. After a few minutes, suddenly, I knew to stop. Looking uncertainly about me, the brilliant sunlight streaming through the bedroom window and across the floor arrested my gaze. Somehow I perceived that his spirit was a part of that light, and he wanted to go with Jesus. I released him in that moment and have never wished him back.

Not many minutes later an ambulance arrived to transport Bill to the hospital – I followed in my car. While we were in route, an emergency room nurse in contact with the ambulance driver recognized the name and alerted the director of nurses that Bill was DOA (dead on arrival). By the time I entered the emergency room doors, the director of nurses, the head nurse from my floor, and several nursing friends were waiting to receive me. With them was Reverend Sanders. How had he arrived before me? I later learned that the ambulance driver, who was a member of our church, had recognized us and called him. So I was immediately surrounded by people who cared for me. Even in my shock and grief, I saw the hand of our Father directing my path and gently caring for me.

My head nurse drove me home and another friend followed in my car. My first call was to our closest friends, Van and Emma Jo Thomas. I told them about Bill's death and asked them to come. Then I called our families.

When the Thomases and Sanders arrived, we all discussed the best plan for me. It was decided that if possible, I should fly to Danville that evening. Reverend Sanders called the airport and booked a 5:30 p.m. flight. I called my sister Mary Franklin, and asked if she and her husband Eddie could meet us at the airport.

At my request Van agreed to go the elementary school, tell Susan and Sandy their daddy had died, and bring them home. When they arrived from school, we slipped to their bedroom. I told them everything that had happened that morning and answered all their questions. We cried wrapped in each other's arms.

Emma Jo helped me pack for the trip and Reverend Sanders took us to the airport. In my state of shock all these dear friends guided me through each decision and acted on my behalf. Sometimes "thank you" is insufficient, and this was one of those times.

The forty-five minute flight was my first time of uninterrupted reflection since Bill's death that morning. With the droning jet engine as background noise, I re-lived the day and tried to imagine my life without him. I distinctly remember thinking that the best part of my life was over, that I had no future, no dreams. The girls and I were three shattered lives and there was nothing I could do to change that reality. What would the next years, days, even hours, be like? I particularly dreaded seeing Bill's mother's grief. Bill was the youngest child, born to her later in life, and no one doubted how much she loved him. Then one selfish thought came to me. If the plane crashed, my family would be back together again.

Mary and Eddie met us at the airport. What a comfort they were. But on the hour drive to Danville, I was so numb that I related the day's events without emotion.

When we finally arrived at my mother-in-law's home in Danville, the house was packed with family and friends in the traditional southern way. Upon entering the front door, we were literally engulfed in their severe grief as they surged forward to embrace us. I was thankful to be able to comfort them despite my empty state. I held them and let them cry, gave assurance, and shared the details of the day's events again.

By God's grace sometime during the evening, a sustaining joy sprang up in me as I chose again the way of thanks in the midst of every circumstance – even this one. *"Be joyful always; pray continually; give thanks in all circumstances, for this is God's will for you in Christ Jesus" (I Thessalonians 5:16-18).*

The next morning Susan, Sandy, and I went to the funeral home to see to all the arrangements. The girls were eleven and eight. I can see them now walking hand-in-hand through the rows of caskets, until they finally stopped and said, "We want this one." It was a simple, masculine casket with an antique grey finish; they believed it would honor him. The funeral itself was very much like the casket – simple and honoring.

The Lord moved in my life in profound ways during our week in Danville and this experience is described in detail in the next chapter, "The Way of Joy."

After these days of saying goodbye and closure, Bill's sister Mary flew back to Atlanta to help us adjust to our new lives. We were met at the airport by Reverend Sanders and his wife and taken home to our apartment. I hope I was able to express how much their kindness meant to me – I considered them true friends.

Mary also was a pure blessing that first week home. Her presence took the sting out of those lonely days. We talked and reminisced. She helped me go through Bill's clothes and personal belongings, and I gratefully accepted her help in planning the move back to Danville when school was out.

The next three months were difficult: juggling work and home, making decisions on my own, deciding what was to be moved, and packing boxes. Any one who has lost a spouse will relate to the unavoidable frustrations of the daily routine faced all alone. But through it all, God's grace abounded towards me.

There was one problem that seemed to elude any practical solution. Both of the girls had pet cats. Sandy's kitten, "Christmas," was trainable, but Susan's cat, "Gordon," had come from the animal shelter and wanted to be somewhere else. One day I was so exasperated, I spoke out loud, "What am I to do with this cat?" A moment later I heard a voice from far away, as when hands are cupped around a mouth, encouraging me, "Get a small doghouse." I went straight out and purchased a doghouse and put it out on our second floor apartment terrace. Gordon went in and out the sliding glass door I left ajar for him and contentedly slept atop his new house to the satisfaction of everyone. Even in these small matters the Lord guided me.

As soon as school was out, my brothers-in-law Eddie and Tyson with my brother James drove to Atlanta to move us back to Danville. Once again we were on a new adventure with the Holy Spirit as our Guide.

While packing up Bill's desk, I came across two poems penned just after his salvation. They expressed his inward change and honored his personal and powerful God. Reflecting on their message, I marveled again at all God had done in our lives. How precious these last five years had been; they were a gift beyond all I had imagined. No, I wouldn't have chosen the valley of the shadow of death, but even still, it was well with my soul. God had more than proved His faithfulness.

Lost and Found
B. A. Worley,
November 4, 1968

I rent my garb of inner-self
Tore at my mental hair.
All of my life I'd searched for God,
But missed Him everywhere.

I sought Him in the church - at home
Elsewhere along the way
Each place I looked, He'd been and gone
My thoughts turned to dismay.

Dismayed, but sure He could be found
I went back to my task
Someone must know just where He dwells
But who? Who could I ask?

And then one day I chanced to think
My search had been all wrong.
I'd looked for something tied to space;
I'd sought Him in the throng.

For God can know no bounds or ties;
He has no home as such.
He dwells somewhere beyond the skies
He dwells in each of us.

Paradise Found
B.A. Worley
November 5, 1968

The chill that races up my spine
When wondrous chords are struck,
Is God's own hand upon my back;
A tune His fingers pluck

His gentle laugh is heard at length
In gurgles of a brook;
His happy thoughts are shared with me
In joy found in a book.

His fresh sweet breath blows 'cross my cheek
In breeze of summer night,
The twinkle in His eyes shines forth
In each star's blinking light.

The snowflakes that so gently fall,
Upon my upturned face,
Are tears of joy God shed for me-
A servant of His grace.

During every moment of my crisis, I experienced my Father's grace:

- *Timing:* On the morning Bill went to Heaven, I was not at work and had not left home to do my errands. I was able to hear the sound in the bedroom and go to him. By God's grace I was given the privilege of being with Bill in his last moments.
- *Revelation knowledge (the God-given ability to know something that only He can reveal):* Bill was given a timely word of prophecy so he could prepare for his death. When he died, I was given the privilege of knowing that his spirit was suspended in the Spirit of God, and that Bill desired my permission to go with Jesus. That information was not mine

28

to know unless the Lord revealed it to me. In that moment God alone supplied the grace to let Bill go.

- *Support:* God provided His servants to surround me in the emergency room and care for our girls and me until we were in the arms of our families. To my family and friends: With a grateful heart I thank you for your wealth of kindness and love as I faced this turning point in my life. You were the hands, feet, and heart of Jesus when I needed you most.

I do not know why Bill was healed of alcoholism but not healed of endocarditis. Some things remain a mystery in this life, but I do know that God is good.

"I am persuaded that neither death nor life, nor angels nor principalities nor powers, nor things present nor things to come, nor height nor depth, nor any other created thing, shall be able to separate us from the love of God which is in Christ Jesus our Lord" (Romans 8:38-39).

The Way of Joy

The day after Bill's death and our arrival back to Danville, I was up early and dressed. The first business of the day was to decide how to bring Bill's remains from Atlanta. My options were by hearse or private plane. The private plane was more expensive, but shorter. Bill had been a navigator in the Air Force and loved flying. The thought of flying his remains was a comfort to me, and the shorter time would be helpful in making the other necessary arrangements so that is what I chose.

Preparation for a funeral is never easy; there are so many decisions to make in the midst of the shock and sorrow, but I was comforted throughout the next days by the familiar southern customs of dealing with grief. A large basket of fresh white carnations had been placed on the front porch announcing our loss. There was a guest book atop a wooden podium to the left of the front door to be signed by visitors. Folding chairs were arranged about the living room, providing extra seating, an encouragement for visitors to "come on in and stay awhile." All these "necessities" were provided by Barker's Funeral Home.

The doorbell rang and soon the house was filled with activity. Mrs. Worley's church family from Third Avenue Christian Church, along with many other family and friends, brought every kind of made-from-scratch food imaginable: fried chicken, ham biscuits, potato salad, chicken and dumplings, macaroni and cheese, deviled eggs, lemon chess pie, chocolate meringue pie, coconut cake and much, much more. Many stayed to "help out" and were invited to "fix a plate" and eat with us. Deliveries from the florist arrived often, and the house was soon filled with cut flowers and plants. Those first few days could be compared to an unending family reunion. But beneath the surface was a rip current of grief that found expression in outbursts of tears as each new arrival entered the house.

On the day of the funeral, as I attended to the needs of my children, I was acutely aware of the frailty of my mother-in-law and sister-in-law. Thankfully, I was still filled with an unexplainable joy that I never questioned, but simply accepted with grateful heart. This strength enabled me to share comforting words about Bill's changed life. I assured them that he was with Jesus in Heaven.

The simple funeral was held in the sanctuary of Mount Vernon United Methodist Church in Danville. Seated in the front, I could fully appreciate the beauty of this one hundred-year-old church with its dark stained wood and enormous stained glass windows. It had been five years since I had heard the life-changing sermon on "holiness" in this very room. So much life had happened since that hour.

The new pastor didn't know us personally, so he shared a dry eulogy entirely from our brief conversation the day before: an outline version of Bill's boyhood, young adult life and education through his graduation from seminary. He shared words of sympathy, followed by an organ solo of "How Great Thou Art." As the service ended Mrs. Worley stifled a sob. She was guided down the aisle leaning on her son Ford for support.

At the graveside we said our final goodbyes. Susan removed a single white rose bud from one of the sprays and we turned and walked away from all that was solid and familiar. But I had this assurance: Jesus would never leave us or forsake us.

After the funeral Bill's immediate family gathered at the house. His mother, sister, aunts and uncles shared stories of his life, whole-hearted, first-hand accounts, that enlarged and warmed the impersonal eulogy of the funeral. I sat back and enjoyed their memories, mixing them with my own.

The morning after the funeral as personnel from the funeral home arrived for their belongings, and friends and family came and went, I sat down at the dining room table and wrote thank you notes.

Around noon I received an unexpected telephone call from my mother. My daddy had suffered a heart attack after the funeral and was in the hospital. She had waited to let me know, wanting to have an updated report. He was now stable. I was so grateful that two of my sisters were still in town to help during this emergency.

I left immediately for the hospital. It was difficult to see him pale, short of breath, and very concerned about me, but I was able to assure him that I was okay.

Each time I visited I could see that he was improving. On my last visit he was sitting up in a chair, smiling at me and interested in my future plans. I told him we would move back to Danville in June. I was able to leave assured of his complete recovery. Praise the Lord, He was out of the hospital within two weeks.

The day before we flew back to Atlanta, Bill's mother had errands to do and a hair appointment and his sister was busy with her travel preparations. She had graciously volunteered to fly back to Atlanta with us for a week. The girls were with my family for the day. For the first time since Bill's death, I was alone. Suddenly, without warning, my joy lifted and in its absence an undiluted grief struck full force. I began to sob desperate, destitute tears that I could not control.

Mary had left a car for my use so I decided to revisit all the places Bill and I had lived. Parking at the curb of each home in succession, I reflected on the events they represented, the struggles and joys of our years as a family, weeping almost uncontrollably all the while.

By mid-afternoon I was emotionally exhausted. Hoping to receive comfort, I went to my church. I didn't have an appointment to speak with the pastor so I asked if I could sit in the sanctuary. I was directed to the chapel instead. Here the violent sobs took hold again, no doubt echoing down every corridor. My minister slipped in after a few minutes. He told me I should look at my life at this time as a huge jigsaw puzzle with many pieces missing. As my life progressed, I would put each new piece I found into the picture, and my life would be complete again. Time was the answer. Words of wisdom? Perhaps. Words of comfort? No.

Still searching for solace, I drove on to the cemetery. The fresh grave was still decorated with cut flowers. There I grieved again with acid tears, pouring out my love for my husband. This fresh wave of turbulent emotions was directed to my Heavenly Father.

Finally, I had cried until I had no more tears. Completely spent, I drove back to the house. Dinner preparations were underway, and I realized I had not eaten or had anything to drink all day. I must have looked dreadful. My eyes were so swollen I could hardly see, and I had laryngitis. The family fretted over me, encouraging me to eat something, but I couldn't. I finally drank some iced tea.

My mother and sister Mary brought the girls from Chatham on their way to the hospital to visit my father. Just seeing them briefly was enough to stabilize my emotions. I was grateful to have my family around me. They brought calm after the storm of grief.

That night I knelt down beside my bed to pray. I was a completely emptied vessel. I thought back over the day I had endured. Perhaps this had been a necessary experience in my healing process, but I sensed that it had tipped into grief that was destructive. "Lord, I can't live like this. I have heard of people grieving for years. I will always love him, but I must go on. I have all the responsibility now. I have to keep a job and provide a home for my children." On and on I went, until there was nothing more to say.

And then in the silence the Holy Spirit spoke, "You can choose. You can choose the way of grief or the way of joy." But He also cautioned me, "There is a condition to the way of joy."

I didn't even ask what the condition was. "I choose the way of joy, Lord!"

In that moment by faith I received my Father's provision for my next years. I slept all night and awakened the next morning filled with renewed joy. *"Weeping may endure for a night, but joy comes in the morning"* Psalm 30:5b.

On the flight back to Atlanta, I reflected on the past week. It had been understandably hard, but shining through all the difficulty was God's grace abounding toward me. I did have a future; I would dream new dreams and I would raise my children to the glory of God. I was confident in Him whose love was strengthening me to begin again:

"For I know the thoughts that I think toward you," says the Lord,
"thoughts of peace and not of evil, to give you a future and a hope."
Jeremiah 29:11

"For I will turn their mourning to joy, will comfort them, and make them rejoice rather than sorrow."
Jeremiah 31:13

"Blessed are those who mourn, for they shall be comforted."
Matthew 5:4

I had not asked, but it did not take long for me to learn the condition for the "way of joy." It was simply this: I could not feel sorry for myself or for my children. If I did, grief swept in.

When I was married, my life seemed so connected. After Bill's death it felt stark, lonely, even pitiful. But I found that I couldn't indulge in self-pity or the destructive grief would return in force. Thoughts like "poor me, I don't have a husband," or "the girls don't have a father like other children" were off limits.

I set my mind and heart to live my life in the joy of the Lord and He has supplied sustaining joy to this day.

As I was writing the chapters "Bill's Fleece" and "Set Your House in Order," I was unsettled by the memories of that very difficult time and hindered by tenacious tears like I hadn't experienced in many years.

While talking with Susan over the phone, I shared the effect these stories were having on me. She responded, "You have given this testimony many times; why would it affect you this way now?"

"I don't know."

"Have you asked the Lord about it?"

"I haven't – but I will."

After I hung up the phone, I inquired of the Lord, "What is causing all this emotion?" His answer returned to me swiftly. "You are feeling sorry for yourself."

I have learned and am continuing to learn that self-pity is a destructive force. When I give into it, I slip away from the joy of the Lord, which is my strength, and into self-centered sorrow. I *choose* to *"go to the altar of God, to God my exceeding joy" (Psalm 43:4a).* At His altar I am restored.

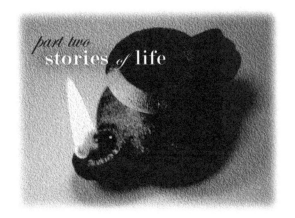

part two
stories *of* life

LIFE is a combination

of the physical functions

of people, animals, and plants.

It is the time between birth and death.

Because God is the source of life,

it is a gift from Him.

Nelson's Illustrated Bible Dictionary[1]

Angels Watching over Me

My spiritual journey is exciting and encouraging. Nothing in this earth life compares to encountering the supernatural as God intervenes in my life. I have experienced His direct guidance, comfort, and miracles – and I also believe I have experienced the ministry of His angels. Each of the following angel stories occurred while I was just living my life, doing normal every-day things. It is interesting that all the stories involve protection while in my car.

As I began writing this chapter, I remembered yet another car incident. This experience precluded my awareness of angel activity. It happened in the late 1960's while Bill was in seminary at Emory University in Atlanta. It was winter. I had taken Bill to an early class and was on my way home. While crossing a two-lane bridge, I hit black ice. The car spun around twice, but stayed in my lane without hitting the bridge or other cars. When it stopped turning, I was headed in the right direction once more and I drove on home. I remember thinking, "That was a miracle!" This story is so similar to the ones that follow I have to wonder if this too was God's intervention through ministering angels.

It was the summer of 1973. Bill had died more than a year before and the girls and I had moved back to Danville. I was working the weekend shift at the hospital and had taken Susan and Sandy to my parent's home on Friday evening. Sunday afternoon after work, I left for Chatham to pick them up.

As I was leaving town, my left back tire began to wobble, so I pulled onto the shoulder of the road. Before I had a chance to get out of my car, a little red sports car pulled up beside me and stopped. A young, African American man dressed in dark suit pants and a sports coat stepped out of his car. Glancing at my tire, he asked, "How far are you going?"

I responded, "About twenty miles."

He advised, "I think you can make it. Drive slowly."

I thanked him and put the car in drive. I envisioned the twenty-mile trip at about 40 mph. To my surprise he pulled out ahead of me, positioned his car directly in front of mine, and set the pace at about 25 mph. I followed his lead, all the while wondering why this young man would take the trouble to drive all the way from Danville to Chatham at that speed. I remember feeling safe and protected, but meanwhile my mind was trying to make sense of the whole situation. "Why would he do this?" Then I heard the Holy Spirit say, "angel of the Lord." I couldn't even begin to process that information; I just accepted it with sincere thanks.

At length we reached the turnoff to my mother's home. I signaled as I turned left off Highway 29 North on to Route 703 to travel the last few miles. I was feeling a little anxious about being on my own, but peace quickly returned and I traveled on without incident at the 25 mph "speed limit."

When I arrived, I got out and looked at the tire. There was a large bubble on the side of it. My brothers George and James were there, so I explained about my tire and asked them to put on the spare. After changing the tire they informed me that there was no way I could have driven from Danville to Chatham on that tire. When they removed it, the large bubble had burst revealing a dry rotted interior.

I was not at the point in my spiritual life that I could talk about supernatural things – like angels, especially with my young adult brothers, and I was still in shock myself. Could it actually be true that we have guardian angels? I didn't dwell on it then, but that's when my perspective changed. I knew from experience that God uses angels.

One Sunday afternoon about ten years later, I was once again on my way from Danville to Chatham. Just as I crested White Oak Mountain, my car-phone rang. As I reached to answer it, I got too close to the right shoulder. In the next instant I hit gravel, over-corrected, and spun out of control into the middle of the highway, turning in circles several times. When the car finally stopped, I realized to my horror that my vehicle was facing on-coming traffic and would not be visible until drivers topped the mountain – way too late for unsuspecting drivers at highway speeds to swerve around me.

Before I could even draw a breath, the car was suddenly pushed *horizontally* to the shoulder of the highway. It came to a stop just as an eighteen-wheeler and a car passed me side by side. The only damage was a slight dent in the left fender from hitting a roadside signpost and a bruised finger.

Somehow, I calmly turned the car around and went on to Chatham. As the shock subsided, joyful bubbled up. I was awed by the love of God in the dawning realization that I have a guardian angel.

Three or four years passed. On this particular day I had been to the mall and grocery shopping. On my way home I spotted Newcomb Carpet and on impulse decided to stop and see my good friend, Janice Newcomb. I'm sure I had something important to tell her.

A left turn is only legal from a separate left lane. It didn't occur to me that I was in the wrong lane until I was mid-turn. Then to my horror, in my peripheral vision I saw a car almost to my door – and I still had two lanes to cross. Instantly I felt strong

41

pressure on top of my right foot, and my car suddenly surged across both lanes safely. Terribly shaken, I stopped long enough to calm down and give thanks to Jesus for His angel in attendance. I didn't visit Janice but went straight home. Strangely, I felt that unusual pressure on the top of my right foot for the next two hours.

This near collision sobered and chastened me. The Holy Spirit showed me that repentance was required. I am now acutely aware of highway rules and regulations and earnestly try to obey them. In my impulsiveness someone may have been seriously injured or killed. I believe that an angel acted on my behalf in my moment of carelessness and stricken terror.

At the time of this next event, perhaps fifteen years later, I was working for a home health agency in Greensboro, North Carolina. This job required driving on back road and byways, areas unfamiliar to me. I can't remember where I was supposed to be going that day, but I dead-ended on the backside of a large, empty parking lot enclosed with wire fencing. I had hardly registered all this, when I drove into a large hole filled with wet mud and gravel and sank up to my car doors on both sides. I couldn't move forward or back or even get out of my car.

I called the office secretary on my car-phone and explained my predicament. As we were talking, I noticed a red pick-up truck turn off the highway and enter the parking lot. It came straight up to me and stopped. The phone was still in my hand, so I told the secretary I thought I had help and would call her back if needs be. A kind grandfatherly, African American man got out of the truck. He was wearing bibbed overalls and a plaid shirt. Without asking if I needed help, he simply said, "I think I can help you." He pulled a chain from the truck bed and expertly hooked it to the back of my car and the front of his truck. Putting my car in reverse, I gassed the petal while he backed my car out of the hole.

As he stowed his chain, I got out of my car to thank him. I wanted to pay him for his service, but he declined. His shiny new truck was now heavily splattered with black mud and gravel. I pleaded to at least be allowed to pay for his truck to be washed, but he refused. All he said before driving off was, "I'll take care of it. There's a car wash close by."

I didn't even have to think about it this time. I knew I had encountered my guardian angel. All I could do was praise and worship my Father for His love and protection.

Over many years in times of crisis and everyday living, the Lord's response to my needs – even when I don't know what to ask – has strengthened my faith.

Some will argue that these events were conjured in my imagination to explain natural phenomenon, that our minds just work that way when we are under pressure or afraid. That is their choice. I choose to believe.

I have also learned that life is precious and not to be handled heedlessly. But even in my foolishness God can rescue me.

angel – member of an order of heavenly beings who are superior to man in power and intelligence. When visible to human beings, angels consistently appear in human form. Sometimes, however, their appearance inspires awe. Angels protect the people of God. They meet a wide variety of human needs, including relieving hunger and thirst and sometimes delivering the people of God from danger (*Nelson's Illustrated Bible Dictionary*).[4]

For He shall give His angels charge over you
to keep you in all your ways.
Psalm 91:11

The angel of the Lord encamps all around those who fear Him,
and delivers them.
Psalm 34:7

Are they not all ministering spirits
sent forth to minister for those who will inherit salvation?
Hebrews 1:14

A Long Walk

In the fall of 1994 I had the privilege of participating in a spiritual retreat called the *Walk to Emmaus* that taught me a lesson I use almost every day: how to serve selflessly and enjoy it. It was a painful lesson to learn, but I share it that those who long to serve others as the Lord serves us may gain from my experience.

The *Walk to Emmaus* (http://emmaus.upperroom.org) is a structured seventy-two hour spiritual retreat offered in many areas of the United States and around the world. There are versions of the same retreat for Catholics, teens, college age, and those in prison. These retreat weekends are generally held in the spring and fall, one for men, and one for women. The purpose of *The Walk to Emmaus* is twofold – to launch personal revival and to return Christians to their local churches better equipped to serve.

It is based on the story in Luke 24:13-31. Two disciples were traveling from Jerusalem to the village of Emmaus the day of Jesus' resurrection. As they traveled together, conversing and reasoning about the troubling events of the past week, Jesus joins them. *"And beginning at Moses and all the Prophets, [Jesus] expounds to them in all the Scriptures the things concerning Himself" (Luke 24:27).* But they did not recognize Him until hours later when He broke the bread at supper. In the same way those who attend the *Walk to Emmaus* set apart time to "walk" with Jesus that He may reveal Himself more fully.

My *Emmaus* retreat was held one hundred miles away from Danville in a repurposed school building complete with dormitory rooms, a dining room, and a bookstore – very comfortable surroundings. We were thirty-two women from all over south-central Virginia spending seventy-two hours away from the cares of the world, to be refreshed in the love of Jesus. We listened to fifteen teachings given by the clergy and lay members of the leadership team, learning deeper truths of God's grace. We became friends as we laughed and cried together.

For me the most meaningful experience of the retreat was taking Holy Communion. Although I had taken Communion many times as a Christian, it was on *The Walk to Emmaus* that I more fully understood how important this symbolic meal is to Jesus, the Host at Table. When I realized how casually I had received the symbols His body and blood, I repented. I now remember the Lord's sacrifice and more fully share in His suffering for sinners like me.

After this rich three-day experience, I returned home overflowing with a new awareness of the fullness of God's love, ready to serve Jesus exuberantly. Soon after, I also knew I wanted to serve at upcoming *Emmaus* retreats, so I sent an application to the *Emmaus* community in my area and was selected to serve on the leadership team of the very next walk (spring of 1995). The bimonthly team meetings would mean traveling two hundred miles round trip, but I eagerly committed nonetheless.

At our first training session, as the director explained the goals of *Emmaus* and outlined the plans for the upcoming retreat, suddenly, I had a brief spiritual vision. This type of experience was new to me. In the vision the Lord highlighted a portion of a Sunday morning twenty years before in the summer of 1973, not

long after Bill's death and our move back to Danville. I had not
thought about this experience since it happened. I was in church
with my daughters Susan and Sandy, ages twelve and ten. At that
time we attended a very formal church. Imagine my surprise,
when at the end of the service, the minister gave an altar call -
the first I ever remembered. And then imagine my terror as the
Holy Spirit strongly prompted me to respond; I knew without a
doubt that I was to go to the altar. My heart was racing as I
instructed the girls to wait in our balcony pew until I came back
for them. I made myself stand up, walk down the steps to the
main level, then travel the length of the formidable aisle to the
altar. I was the only one in the congregation who responded.

The vision was fascinating; I saw myself walking down
the aisle from the perspective of an observer at the back of the
sanctuary. I was wearing a cornflower blue, cotton dress with
short sleeves; the skirt was paneled and flared slightly as I
walked. I had forgotten all about that dress. I watched myself
arrive at the altar, remembering that as I knelt, I had no idea why
I was there. At that moment I had no pressing problems – just
life in general. Having responded to the Spirit's prompting, I
heard nothing from God, so I prayed a brief prayer that His will
would be done in my life. Of course I still had to face the long
aisle back to my seat with all those curious eyes looking at me.
After a few moments the scene in the vision faded and I was
aware again of the *Emmaus* orientation. Then the Holy Spirit
spoke, "For this, for *The Walk to Emmaus*, you went to the altar
that Sunday."

I had been chosen for service in the *Emmaus* movement
and accepted the call more than twenty years ago? I was
astounded. As if in confirmation, I suddenly remembered the gift
Susan had sent as a remembrance for my *Emmaus* retreat several
months earlier. It was a hand-made, fabric banner appliqued with
a hen and two chicks (roosters, hens and chicks are *Emmaus*
symbols.) The attached note had read, "For such a time as this." I
knew most certainly that I had been called to this very moment
and this specific ministry as a sovereign direction for my life.

The vision was a glorious revelation, but what followed was the opposite of my expectations. One of the foundational principles of *Emmaus* is leadership through anonymous servant hood. I had always enjoyed serving, but I was about to be deeply immersed in the unwelcome school of true humility.

It all began on the day the leadership team received specific assignments for the upcoming retreat. All my Danville friends were given one of the fifteen teachings or decorating the chapel or some other seemingly glamorous job. My assignment was to be separated to the kitchen to prepare snacks for everyone else. What a waste of my people skills and spiritual wisdom! An isolated, insignificant job was certainly not one of the things I wanted to do. I wanted to do something influential. I wanted to be noticed. I mostly wanted to be *needed*. (My reasons for this emotionally depleted state in this season of my life come into the story in my next chapters.)

My disappointment gave the enemy an open place to attack and he came swiftly to insinuate that I had been separated from the rest of the team because I was only worthy of kitchen work. (This should have been humorous since I had always liked the kitchen and was a good cook.) I tried to resist and put on my best face, but inside I felt left out and unworthy of a speaking part. Wasn't I as spiritual as everyone else? On and on this enemy prompted self-talk went until misery settled in. I did push through enough to do the best job I could, putting extra effort into it, and didn't complain aloud, but my heart was not in it.

I served on the leadership team for the next several retreats in the same position and crestfallen state of mind. On the third retreat I was finally assigned a teaching. But it didn't go well. I couldn't express what I wanted to say. I felt ill equipped. Insecure and vulnerable, I didn't ask for help and the whole teaching fell short of my hopes. Now I was more miserable than ever.

Over the next several years I was assigned more teachings, but felt I never "performed" well. I knew something was wrong but had no idea what it was. I don't remember reaching out to friends, or even asking Jesus for help. I think I was in a season of self-sufficiency and making do – and it wasn't working. Eventually, I gave up on my goal to dazzle and settled in to do the best I could. This forlorn plodding went on and on.

It took many years, but one day I realized with a start that I had learned to graciously serve no matter what the assignment and here was the key: As I rested in the Lord's affection for me and my confidence in Him, He faithfully provided the grace to rejoice with my friends – all good speakers and very creative in their assignments. Encouraging my friends, praying for them before their teachings, gradually shifted my focus from my miserable self to the delight of undergirding others. Free of my self-talk and the lies of the enemy, I was no longer concerned with the showiness of my assignments or how my attempts to speak were perceived. I rejoiced instead in the unified service of the whole leadership team as we blessed those who attended the retreats. I had finally broken through to the goal of anonymous servanthood.

I praise my Father for His perseverance in my life, as I made the long walk through the school of humility to selfless love, His life lesson for me.

As I was writing this story, I asked the Lord why I was required to go to the altar so many years before *The Walk to Emmaus*. He explained, "I wanted you to receive humility, and this was your first step." Suddenly, I remembered the insecure and vulnerable feeling of walking down the isle to the altar. God Himself had given me the courage to step out and obey despite my fear of what people would think. It had been a fitting parallel for the insecure and vulnerable *Emmaus* experience. But reflecting on the length of the journey and the pain of the lesson learned, I rejoiced. It had all been worth it. I have found my true self through serving.

I have learned that God really loves me; He cares about my character and spiritual growth more than I do. I am being made into the image of Jesus as He continues to lead me down the "Emmaus Road," walking by my side, expounding the scriptures to me.

I have also found that true humility doesn't produce pride – it produces gratitude. And our service to others is an expression of our confidence in Him. Our unified service to God is beautiful and powerful.

humility – a freedom from arrogance that grows out of the recognition that all we have and are comes from God (*Nelson's Illustrated Bible Dictionary*)[5]

My son, do not despise the chastening of the Lord
nor be discouraged when you are rebuked by Him
For whom the Lord loves He chastens,
and scourges every son whom He receives.
Hebrews 12:5-6

Stay Away from a Foolish Man

After Bill's death in March of 1972, Susan, Sandy and I moved back to Danville, Virginia to be close to our family and settled into our new lives. As Bill suggested, I built a house. It was just down the street and around the corner from the house we had lived in before the move to Atlanta – the one we thought would never sell. I supported the family by nursing at Danville Memorial Hospital. The Lord provided grace to raise my girls. I was content in my singleness. Yes, I missed Bill, but I was not lonely. With school days and family activities five good years passed.

Then a surprise! During the Christmas season of 1977, I received an unexpected Christmas card from an old boy friend. I had met Rice Strange in December 1955 during my first year in nursing school. Rice was tall, redheaded and fun to be with. He was readily adopted into my circle of family and friends and I into his. It was not long before I realized I was falling in love.

Rice and I dated until my senior year, but after he left school to join the army, we drifted apart and eventually married other people. I had not seen or heard from him since. I was genuinely delighted to receive his Christmas card.

A few weeks later we met for dinner and caught up on each other's lives. He was an industrial engineer. He told me he had been divorced for three years and had a daughter and a son. I was glad to hear that he was a member of First Presbyterian Church in Danville, and was attending a prayer group there. His hobby was racing jeeps and judging by his many trophies, he was good at it. He also enjoyed working on cars.

From that evening the relationship accelerated rapidly – perhaps too rapidly. We began dating in January and Rice proposed in March. We were married on June 3, 1978 (in the quaint Methodist church where Bill and I had been married eighteen years before) and spent a romantic honeymoon in the U.S. Virgin Islands.

Our union created a blended family with four teens: my daughters were seventeen and fifteen. His daughter Ann was sixteen, and his son Rice, Jr. was thirteen.

Rice was living in a spacious, fifty-year-old, log cabin that had been his parent's summer home. It was delightfully situated on wooded acreage just over the Virginia border in Pelham, North Carolina. So it was decided that we would sell my house in Danville and begin our married life there.

I joined Rice's church in the next weeks. We attended various prayer groups and Bible studies, fellowshipping frequently with other couples. We even served on a mission trip to Trinidad.

If I could summarize my next twenty-three years with Rice, I would call it an adventure of two types: It was an adventure in the sense that I did thrilling things and went to interesting places. But the adventure also took me to my knees in relational pain and taught me some of the most difficult, but valuable spiritual lessons of my life. Some of these lessons I will share in the next chapters. In this story I want to honor the Lord, who strengthened me and faithfully directed me all the way through this marriage to a place of peace on the other side.

In the beginning life was good – most of the time. But we had been married only a few weeks when I began to feel troubled. We had a definite communication problem and there were other vague issues I couldn't identify.

As the months stretched into years, I discovered a paradox in Rice's personality. On the one hand he had never grown up. His attire and hairstyle were reminiscent of the sixties. His perception of people and situations remained as narrow and self-centered as a teenager's, his manners unpolished. Yet, he was very intelligent, a hard worker, and loved to learn. Rice never hesitated to invest in the latest technology or gadgets for his auto shop hobby. He also had a gift for financial investments. But Rice reveled in these personal pursuits with little genuine interest in the people around him – even me. This inability to have deep relationships was the most troubling aspect of life with Rice.

In addition Rice's words were seldom edifying. He had an explosive anger problem that erupted occasionally at unexpected moments, raining hurtful words on whoever happened to be assembled. At other times his comments were tinged with prejudice or lewdness. He never asked for forgiveness – not even once – and as a result he left damaged relationships all around him.

I was grieved about these tendencies, but rarely confronted him. Everything was O.K. most of the time, so I just let troubling behavior go. I did the dirty work of soothing hurt feelings after his occasional tirades and hurried back to the peaceful routine of life A.S.A.P. Denial was my way of coping. To my sorrow, I know now that I enabled Rice's immaturity and selfishness by sidestepping confrontation. *This was definitely not good.*

But I also clung to the principles of love (I Corinthians 13). As an act of my will, I refused to become bitter and purposed to forgive Rice for his selfish choices and destructive outbursts. I kept the vision for who Rice was becoming in my heart. I believed in him, hoped for him, and was patient with him. I wanted a home where the love of God prevailed and I was willing to sacrifice to that end. I firmly believed in the sanctity of the marriage covenant and was committed to Rice whatever the cost. *This was good.*

As the years passed, our teenagers finished their education and married or started their careers. Rice traveled for his work all of our marriage and was usually away three to four days a week. He also traveled internationally. Sometimes I traveled with him. We visited Boston, Jamaica, Mexico, and Canada. I had always wanted to travel, but had never had the means or freedom to do so. These were special trips and helped our relationship.

In our next adventure Rice decided to buy a small airplane, take pilot lessons, and become licensed. He succeeded and then encouraged me to take lessons too. I had never imagined flying a plane, but I eventually soloed. It was an exhilarating experience! However, when I took the test to get my pilot's license, I didn't pass. I was satisfied to know I could land the plane in an emergency.

We enjoyed flying places in half the driving time. We flew to Nashville for the World's Fair. We flew to Oklahoma several times to visit Susan and her family. Once we took his daughter Anne to Williamsburg to shop.

Later Rice found a seaplane and traded for it. Now we could fly to our small lake property, land on the lake and taxi up to our dock. Soon we were flying back and forth to the lake on the weekends. Our children sometimes joined us. These were special family times.

Eventually Rice's fervor for planes waned and a passion for boats and fishing rose and took its place. Rice had loved fishing his whole adult life. The highlight of every year was a week of fishing with his co-workers at Cape Hatteras, N.C. When he retired at age fifty-five, he bought a fishing boat and a small, inland house in Beaufort, N.C. Soon he was fulfilling a lifelong dream of becoming a commercial fisherman. He now divided his time between the beach and the lake, visiting home only two or three days a week. I still worked full time, so I joined him as I could. But when I made the effort to be with him, I began to feel less and less welcome.

One weekend I was at the beach and found several pieces of female clothing in the dryer. I confronted Rice, but he claimed to know nothing about them. His only comment was, "You're the only woman here; if they're not yours, I don't know whose they are."

More problems surfaced, mostly concerning my children, grandchildren, and extended family. Rice didn't want my family visiting our home. When they did, he was sullen, even outwardly rude. I was miserable,

We were definitely on two different paths. Direct conversations with my Heavenly Father were my lifeline. I knew from experience that prayer changes the events of our lives and ultimately the core of who we are, so I persevered in my marriage, trusting that God was at work. I re-doubled my effort to love my husband through God's love for me. I prayed all the time.

Rice now spent two or three days a week at home and three or four at the beach. Sometimes he stayed all week without coming home, and once he stayed two weeks. Honestly, it was easier for me when he was away as I could enjoy my family.

In July 1998 Rice called me to confirm the time I would join him at our beach house for the Fourth of July celebration. The caller ID showed a woman's name – *June*. I asked Rice about it and he told me he was at her home working on her car when he remembered he needed to call me. But I didn't believe him and decided to stay home for the Fourth instead.

A few months later on the weekend of my sixtieth birthday, my sister Patricia joined us at the beach to celebrate. Things were strange and strained. For the first time in our married lives, Rice did the cooking. I was amazed. When I examined the cookbook he was using, obviously a fund-raising type, I found that a woman named *June* had submitted the recipe he was using. This was my final clue: Rice was deeply involved in an affair. Still I didn't confront him. Every time I decided to open the conversation, I began to doubt if I had all the facts. Looking back I have to wonder at my naivety.

It was Christmas Day that year when I finally accepted that my husband no longer loved me. My gift from him that year was a hubcap for my car. I was shocked and hurt. For the sake of his children, who were with us that morning, I expressed exuberant thanks for the gift and made it through the day – and then the tears came.

In these next days I finally removed the rose-colored glasses and took an honest look at the last twenty-three years. As I did, I saw the truth: All the traveling and lewd insinuations, the lack of intentionality in our relationship – this was not Rice's first extra-marital affair, but probably one of many from the first years of our marriage. Here finally was the elusive, missing information that made everything else make sense.

It was then that the Lord released me from my marriage. But this injunction caused a moral dilemma. I knew that He also hates divorce. My commitment to marriage was so strong – for better or for worse until death. But I also knew Rice's adultery released me from my vows. One day I was sure I was to leave, and the next, no, I would stay. I was so conflicted I was unable to move in any direction.

One Saturday in January, Rice came in for lunch and sat down at the kitchen table, complaining of extreme weakness. He had needed to rest for long periods of time during the morning. On Monday he called his physician who conducted testing and informed him that he had suffered a silent heart attack at some previous time and had heart damage. On February 23 Rice had a successful triple bypass surgery. He recovered well, but our relationship was strained to the limit. In early March he had one of his friends drive him to the beach "to check on things."

While Rice was away, I reassessed my situation. An optimist at heart, I reasoned that if Rice could move past his denial about his relationship with June and repent, we could talk through the problems in our relationship and start again. I also took an honest evaluation of my life. Nothing is one-sided. I genuinely wanted to understand my contribution to our problems. I was willing to change to be what he needed, but as far as I could discern my conscience was clear. Looking back I see that my sin was conflict avoidance and fear of Rice's manipulative temper.

In June 1999, Rice came home for the week for our twenty-third wedding anniversary. We went out for dinner to celebrate. During the meal I lifted my glass and toasted, "To us." Rice's glass was already raised as I offered the toast. At my words he set his glass on the table without a word. His choice was made.

Such anguish. Such indecision. I was restless all day long and wasn't sleeping at night. At around 4:00 a.m., June 10, I slipped out to the front porch. Swinging gently on our antique, wicker swing, I half listened to the tree frogs and prayed fervently. At last the Holy Spirit got through to me. I *knew* I was to leave Rice – that very day.

Still I needed a confirmation that was so clear I would know the rest of my life that He had directed me to leave. "Lord, please confirm Your spoken Word with Your written Word." I went back into the house to get my Bible. Holding it closed in both hands, I let it fall open. (This way of hearing from the Lord was unusual for me, but desperate situations call for desperate means.) As it opened, my eyes fell on these words: *"Stay away from a foolish man, for you will not find wisdom on his lips . . . Fools mock at making amends for sin" (Proverbs 14:7 – 9).* That was all the confirmation I needed. I no longer wavered. I was to leave.

Rice got up around 8:00 o'clock that morning. I waited until he drank about a half-cup of coffee, then challenged him, "You have not asked me to forgive you for your relationship with June."

He responded, "There is nothing to forgive. I've done nothing wrong."

There it was from his own mouth, *"Fools mock at making amends for sin."* There was no doubt of my next step. "Well, that's it for me," I said standing to my feet. "I'm leaving you."

"Where are you going?"

"To the Stratford Inn."

"Well," he slowly responded, "There is no need for that expense or for you to leave the house. I'll leave."

Rice spent the day packing. We had no conversation.

That evening when he was ready to leave, I walked him to his car. His casual parting comment was, "I figure I have ten more years to live. My dad lived ten years after his heart attack." Then he drove away.

I grieved my marriage and continued to pray for Rice and June until his death on January 25, 2002, two and a half years later.

As I trusted God, I found Him faithful to bring me all the way through this very painful experience. But I can also see that I enabled my husband to continue in his lifestyle because I was too afraid to examine the signs and confront his sin. I depended on God to do His part, but I only partially did mine.

I have learned that love for others has many facets and is always a choice. True love is powerful. It is kind. It believes the best of others. It practices forgiveness. God blesses our sacrifices for love's sake.

We cannot change anyone else, but we can change ourselves. In the end, each of us is responsible to God alone for the way we live our lives. The Holy Spirit is patient with us, wooing us to Himself. But there comes a time when each of us must appear before the Lord. We should not put off repentance and salvation. The time is shorter than we think.

As We Forgive Our Debtors

For many years after my salvation experience, forgiving was easy. I had grasped the work of the cross by Jesus for the forgiveness of my sins (as much as so great a grace can be grasped). I also knew to freely forgive others, and did so as much as I knew how. But the day came when the Lord plunged me deeper into the discipline of forgiveness.

I don't remember the exact year of this significant incident in my life; I think the late 1980's or early 1990's. I know for sure it was the week before Mother's Day. On Monday morning as my husband Rice prepared to leave for several days of out of town work, I mentioned the upcoming holiday and suggested that we celebrate Mother's Day with a family dinner at our house. He asked who would be coming. I named all of my immediate family in the area. He then flatly stated which ones he didn't want to come.

If he had stabbed me point blank where I stood, my inner being could not have been more stricken. I could barely breathe. The pain was so great I couldn't respond so I stood mute and motionless as he walked out the door, got into his car, and drove away. I couldn't even cry.

Here was the evidence of what I had suspected: I had welcomed his family into my heart from the beginning, but after many years of marriage, Rice's heart was still resolutely cold towards those I loved most, those who were the joy of my life.

Rice had expressed many unkind attitudes and I had lived with them relatively well until this moment. Why did this one conversation hurt so much? Looking back, I can see that this was a turning point in our relationship - perhaps the beginning of the end. Rice didn't love my family. He wasn't even willing to tolerate them. If he couldn't love my family, how could he love me?

Profound sorrow and loss washed in behind this revelation and shock set in. Three days passed and the pain remained acute. I went to work, but was barely able to make it through the day. I felt that my very life was being drained out of me. I had heard of people dying of a broken heart, and now I saw how that could happen.

When I arrived home from work on Wednesday evening, the house was drab, cold and lifeless – just like me – so I decided to stoke the fire to knock the spring chill off the family room. Opening the black iron doors of the woodstove, I peered in and saw I would need kindling. Setting my purse on the coffee table, I headed out to the woodpile. But the pain in my tortured heart was so unbearable that having arrived, all I could do was stand and stare. I had reached an emotional precipice. I couldn't go on. Desperately, I cried out loud to my God and Father, my most trusted Confidante, "I can't live like this any longer!"

In the next moment I heard His firm, but kind voice in answer, "The sin is against you, not against Me; you do something about it."

His voice was not the familiar "still small" inner voice of my past experience. It was audible. (I believe this was the only time I have ever heard Him speak audibly.) The sound seemed to come from the opposite side of the woodpile, a little higher than my head.

Turning the phrase in my mind, I realized the Lord was right. Rice had not specifically said anything against God – even though each of us must eventually answer to God for our relationships. Rice had spoken against my family and me. Up until this moment, I had believed that although we could hurt one another, all true sin was committed against God alone. I was so taken aback that I physically stepped backward.

"Well, Lord, I'm not sure that what Rice has done can be called a *sin*."

In a stronger tone the Lord repeated, "The sin is against you, not against Me. You do something about it."

Bursting into tears, I sobbed, "I don't know what to do about sin against me."

Suddenly, a portion of God's Word came into my mind, something about forgiving the sins of others. I thought it was in the book of *John*.

Kindling forgotten, I rushed into the house, opened my Bible on the desk, and found the passage. Jesus was preparing to ascend into Heaven and was instructing His disciples: "*'Peace to you. As the Father has sent me, I also send you.' And when He had said this, He breathed on them, and said to them, 'Receive the Holy Spirit. If you forgive the sins of any, they are forgiven them: If you retain the sins of any, they are retained.'" (John 20:21-23)*.

With tears still streaming, I confessed, "I don't know how to forgive sin against me."

Patiently, my Father replied, "How do *I* forgive sin?"

"With the blood of Jesus," I answered promptly.

Then God confirmed, "That is how *you* forgive sin."

So, with the precious blood of the Lamb, I covered Rice's words by deliberately speaking aloud, "With the blood of Jesus I forgive you, Rice." As I spoke the words, the pain left, and I took a deep breath – the first in three days. Simultaneously, in my spirit I watched Rice's words against my family and me split in half and separate to the east and west. Those words never had the power to hurt me again.

For the next several hours the Holy Spirit continued His ministry of healing over many wounding incidents from my past. The hurtful words or actions of my parents, siblings, grandparents, and others were brought to my memory one at a time in random order. By intentionally speaking their names aloud and covering their specific sin with the blood of Jesus, I forgave each one. What a powerful transformation! This was one of the most significant revelations of my life.

I am eternally grateful to be forgiven for my sins against God and others. I also rejoice in the authority to forgive my "debtors," those who sin against me. *Then Peter came to Him and said, 'Lord how often shall my brother sin against me and I forgive him? Up to seven times?' Jesus said to him, 'I do not say to you up to seven times, but up to seventy times seven'* (Matthew 18:21-22).

Ten years passed with "seven times seventy" opportunities to practice covering sins against me with the blood of Jesus before my next major test case was at hand. By this time I knew that there was something foundationally wrong with my marriage. As I shared in the last chapter, my suspicion that Rice was having an affair was eventually confirmed and we had separated in June 1999.

It was now April of the next year, and I was preparing to be a team member once more for *The Walk to Emmaus*. As I ironed clothing to pack for the weekend retreat, I sincerely prayed aloud for Rice, using the traditional Emmaus Prayer to the Holy Spirit as a guide:

> Come Holy Spirit, fill the hearts of Your faithful
> and kindle in [Rice] the fire of Your love.
> Send forth Your Spirit and [he] shall be created
> and You shall renew the face of the earth.
> O God, who by the light of the Holy Spirit
> did instruct the hearts of the faithful,
> Grant that by the same Holy Spirit
> [Rice] may be truly wise
> and ever enjoy Your consolations
> through Christ our Lord.[6]

As I finished praying for him, the Holy Spirit asked, "What about June?" Surprised by the question, I stood there, iron in hand, and considered, "What about June?" I had already forgiven her and mailed a note telling her so. Wasn't that enough?

In the next instant God allowed me to experience a larger sense of His huge heart of love for June. I understood that God wanted me to continue to pray for those I forgave. Oh how He loves! Setting the iron down, I earnestly prayed for June, allowing God's pure love to pour through me to her. I specifically prayed for her soul, her health, and her family. After that praying for both Rice *and* June became my habit.

About a year and a half later, on Friday, January 25, 2002, a friend of Rice's called me at work with word that Rice had suffered a heart attack and died that morning. I immediately called the hospital in Morehead City, North Carolina. The ER doctor confirmed that Rice had suffered a massive heart attack and was dead on arrival, then added sympathetically, "His fiancée is still here. Do you want to speak with her?" Feeling suddenly drained, I replied, "No, I'm his wife," and hung up the phone. Though numb with the unexpected news, I was more relieved that the marriage was finally over, than grieved over Rice's death.

When I arrived home about fifteen minutes later, I began making the necessary phone calls. Rice's sister-in-law, my dear friend Carol Strange offered to help make the arrangements. I gratefully accepted and left immediately for her home. Late in the afternoon Rice, Jr., and I left for Beaufort (about four hours away) to meet with June and get Rice's burial clothes.

All I could do was praise God in the highest; I sat talking with June that evening with no jealousy or bitterness – only God's compassion flowing through me. In the course of the conversation it seemed natural to ask if she wanted to come to the funeral. She burst into tears and acknowledged that she did want to come and would arrive Sunday morning. Going a step further, I invited her and her family to have lunch at my home before the service.

Saturday evening after visitation at the funeral home, Rice's daughter Ann and I had a few moments alone. As we reminisced, Ann remarked, "Have you ever heard of a funeral with a wife, an ex-wife, and a fiancée' all in attendance?" We had a good laugh at the complexity – even absurdity of the situation. Oh how good it was to laugh. With the laughter I was aware of God's love enveloping us. For me it was freeing. *"A merry heart does good, like medicine" (Proverbs 17:22).*

June and her family arrived as expected on Sunday. Ann, Susan and I served their lunch and visited with them while they ate. The sting of the affair had no power to hurt me. Peace prevailed, love reigned, and I rejoiced!

———————————

Understanding the power and practicality of the blood of Jesus is one of the most important components of my journey through life. When we grasp that we are forgiven for our past, present, and future sins, we are equipped to forgive others over and beyond for each offense against us. They are connected.

Forgiving others doesn't mean that those who sin against us are not responsible for their attitudes and actions before God. It does mean that they don't owe us anything anymore and their offenses do not hold us in bondage. The blood of Jesus is that powerful and that available for our use.

Our Father in heaven . . .
forgive us our debts as we forgive our debtors
Matthew 6:9, 12

I canceled all that debt of yours because you begged me to.
Shouldn't you have had mercy on your fellow servant just as I
had on you?
Matthew 18:32b – 33

Therefore as the elect of God, holy and beloved, put on
tender mercies, kindness, humility, meekness, long suffering,
bearing with one another, if anyone has a complaint against
another, even as Christ forgave you, so you also must do.
Colossians 3:12

Roses for My Birthday

I've always loved my September 1st birthday. According to my mother, I was born on Labor Day, so every year my celebration is somewhere near the holiday weekend, and often includes a picnic or family gathering before the beginning of school.

But I was dreading this, my 62nd birthday (1999). Rice and I had separated in June. In the next months my usual confidence and optimism were replaced with failure and rejection. In this depleted place my echoing question became, "Am I loved?"

Let me explain. There was no doubt in my *mind* that God loved me, as did my family and many friends. But my *heart* was aching and I yearned for tangible reassurance. So I asked my Father in Heaven and Him alone for a very specific birthday present. I asked for roses for my birthday.

September 1st arrived, a sparkling day filled with promise. At 8 a.m. the doorbell rang and there stood my daughter Sandy with a bouquet of fresh flowers – but no roses. She had come to take me to breakfast as a surprise, a delightful way to start the day.

Throughout the next hours I received phone calls from family and friends and the mailbox held many birthday cards. In the afternoon a florist truck arrived with flowers from my sister Dorothy. It was a lovely arrangement of fall flowers – but no roses.

Around 4:30 p.m. I left for the Greensboro airport to meet Susan, who was flying in from Tulsa to spend a few days. As I waited for her to exit the plane (these were the days when you could go all the way to the gate), I fully expected to see a rose or two in her hand. She disembarked with her backpack – but no roses.

On the hour's drive home Susan and I laughed and talked, sharing our lives. I was thankful for my daughters, who were helping me through this difficult time. But simultaneously in my spirit, I was conversing with my Father. "Lord, I know You are able to place roses on my pillow. Nothing is too hard for You." I smile now at my unshakable faith. I was confident I would receive roses that day.

We arrived home at 7 p.m. Sandy had come over with her family and prepared our favorite family dinner, a southern feast: fried chicken, creamed potatoes, biscuits, gravy, macaroni and cheese, green beans, and of course birthday cake.

As I entered the living room – surprise! surprise! There on the coffee table was a large glass vase filled with thirty beautifully arranged garden roses. The colors were breathtaking in shades of yellow, pink and red. And oh, the fragrance! Only fresh garden roses are perfumed like that. Even though I had fully expected roses from my Father on my birthday, I was stunned at their presence and beauty, overwhelmed with His extravagant love.

As it turned out, my sister-in-law Carol had cut these roses from her own rose garden, artistically arranged them, and delivered them in person while I was at the airport. That she, Rice's sister-in-law, was the one who brought my Father's birthday gift, blessed me more than I can describe. I held love in my hands and I knew it.

I have heard all my life that God provides for our needs, not our wants. That may be true in some cases, but I have learned that He sometimes places desires in our hearts because we need them.

A Gathering Place

After Rice's death in January 2002, I continued living in our home in Pelham, North Carolina, an old log house on large acreage, working in nearby Yanceyville as a home health nurse. I loved the property and every log of that old house, but it was not really mine. It had been willed to Rice's son at his death. And although I had been invited to continue living on the property for a season, by the summer of 2004 I had become restless. I wanted a home of my own.

I had moved many times and knew that the logistics of moving were a tremendous undertaking. In my journal I began to voice earnest prayers for a new home and the guidance of the Lord in securing it.

As I prayed, I also considered my options for location. Moving near one of my siblings was a delightful possibility, but in the end I felt most peaceful about moving back to Danville just over the state line. It would be convenient to be in town near my closest friends with church minutes away. Work would be about the same distance as well. I pursued this direction as I was able, driving through neighborhoods searching for "for sale" signs. I looked for weeks but found nothing.

As I sought the Lord's guidance for a house just right for me, He brought to mind Matthew 5:14-16 which begins, *"You are the light of the world."* Jesus didn't want me to place my light under a bushel, but on a stand where it would be *"light for the whole house."* Then I heard the Holy Spirit say, "You are light. Come out from under the cares of the world, so others can see your light and glorify your Father in Heaven." When God speaks it is so rich and personal and it changes our perspective. I began to see myself as a lamp, filled with the oil of the Holy Spirit and able to give light to others. As the revelation unfolded – it took several months to fully discern – I realized that my new home was to be the center of my Spirit-filled ministry.

Now I knew it was the Lord's will for me to move and how He would use my new home. But I still had no home to move into or clear direction about how to find one. I struggled with initiative at this juncture. Overwhelmed, I shut down instead of moving forward.

One October evening as I was turning onto Goodman Road, all but home, I received an unexpected gift. On my right across the adjoining field was the highest, most perfectly arched rainbow I had ever seen. An October rainbow – how unusual! It was so striking I slowed to fully absorb the scene. The colors were pale, but vivid. End to end it seemed to touch the ground on both sides. I thought, "Two pots of gold!" and then, "It must have rained somewhere." As I turned into my driveway, I stopped once more and looked back. What a privilege.

This glimpse of glory seemed to lift my eyes to the One who makes and keeps promises. In the next weeks the memory of that rainbow somehow intertwined with my request for a new home and planted hope deep within me. It is difficult to explain how I knew that God was reassuring me, but after this experience whenever I felt discouraged, unexpectedly, I remembered the rainbow and fresh hope returned.

On a cold November morning a few weeks later, as I rounded a curve on Old Highway 29, I was startled and awed by a second rainbow. This one was hanging low in the sky broad and brilliant, like a banner. With the unexpected sight came a single word: *promise*. All day I meditated on those breathtaking rainbows and wondered at the word "promise" that had been quickened to me by the Holy Spirit. Suddenly I knew I was to move forward in the search for a new home.

The very next day I called a realtor and we talked at length about the area I was most interested in and my price range, setting a date to meet in person. In early December, I met with Janice Chapman and liked her right away. She was friendly, efficient, and trustworthy. That day we looked at several houses, but none interested me. With the Christmas season approaching, we agreed to continue house shopping at the first of the year.

Promptly in the first week in January 2005, Janice called with new housing possibilities for me to see. I was excited. After that Friday afternoons became our time to look at prospective homes, sometimes seeing at as many as five houses in those hours together. But I couldn't envision myself living in any of them.

One Friday when we had finished seeing all the houses on her list, Janice asked if I was interested in going to dinner. I certainly was, and we added dinner to our Friday night house-hunting adventure. We were new best friends and the friendship has continued to this day.

Now that I was in the midst of focused, persistent house hunting my general prayers about a home of my own gradually sharpened to specific. The more I searched, the more the Lord helped me understand what I wanted and needed in a home. Those with the spiritual gift of hospitality will appreciate my checklist.

The location of the kitchen was the first consideration. In the log home the kitchen and living areas were on opposite ends; I was not willing to be separated from family and friends in my new home. I also wanted inviting rooms that flowed into one another with plenty of space for all my antique furniture and twelve-seat dining room table. Another necessity was enough space for children, grandchildren (I have thirteen) and others to visit overnight. And even though I knew a one-level house was probably more sensible at this point in my life, my heart's desire was for a two-story home with a spacious front porch and a small, manageable yard. If the whole dream home could be summarized, what I wanted with all my heart was a *gathering place* - a home where hospitality reigned. Did such a wondrous house even exist and equally as important: Was it possible on my budget?

As I continued praying, I included Janice in my prayers. I prayed that the Lord would give her His guidance to find the house He had for me. I also asked that she would receive a good commission for her hard work.

Searching, searching, searching. We had scoured south Danville, so now we moved to the north side. But again through all those Friday afternoons, I didn't see a single house I could imagine as my own.

One Friday in April after viewing all of the houses on Janice's list, she mentioned, "There is a house on West Main Street, new on the market. It's over budget, but do you want to look at it?" At my affirmative she made an appointment for the next afternoon.

Making our way to the house that Saturday, I surveyed the area with pleasure. I had always liked historic south Danville, lined with large older homes all in a row, almost condominium cozy. Yes, this street was a main thoroughfare, but just two-lane and winding.

Parking at the curb, I stood on a sidewalk lined with ancient trees in front of a three-story red brick home with white columns. Much of this almost one hundred year-old home seemed to be restored. The windows were framed with the original black shutters on hinges. Broad brick stairs led up to a porch the width of the house. There was even a white porch swing. And how lovely – the wide, black door was framed with white latticework and windowpanes in the manner of bygone years. The house invited us to "come on in."

We entered a spacious foyer with a twelve-foot ceiling. Janice pointed out the hand-painted diamond design on the walls and the original wood staircase just ahead. To the left and right were matching French doors and symmetrical rooms with fireplaces visible from the foyer.

On the left was a dining room and to the right a formal living room. Choosing right we entered the living room and turned left through a third set of French doors into the adjoining family room, passing on into the adequate kitchen across the back of the house. A winning added feature was a screened-in porch off the kitchen facing the backyard. From there the rooms circled back. First, there was a full bath then a laundry room tucked under the staircase landing. A little further on was a room used as an office, and we were back at the dining room that I had glimpsed from the foyer as we came in. All the downstairs rooms, though smallish, flowed into one another without the need for hallways. With the ten-foot ceilings, the combined effect felt easy and open.

Upstairs were six bedrooms and two full baths. The two bedrooms that faced the street had fireplaces, an extension of the chimney flue just below them. Above the bedrooms was a dusty, unfinished attic with two windows facing the street.

The first and second stories had original hardwood floors, wonderfully preserved. The house had central heat, and unusual for these older homes – central air. If these features were not enough, the backyard was small and the front yard smaller. Perfect. I loved this house! Janice submitted my speedy, modest offer, but it was understandably rejected.

Back to our mission, we continued our weekly search until Janice called one day in May. "There is another house for sale on West Main Street and the one you liked is still available and has been reduced in price. Do you want to look at it again?"

"Definitely, yes!"

I called my sister-in-law Carol and asked if she would meet us there. Again, I could see myself in this house with my family gathered and grandchildren everywhere. Carol thought the house was in good condition and not overpriced.

The second house, just up the street, was smaller and needed a lot of repairs, but the price was much lower. I went home and committed this decision to the Lord. In prayer, I laid down what I wanted in exchange for what my Father wanted for me.

The following Saturday, Sandy and her husband Rodney met with us to compare both houses. Back in the car, I asked what they thought. Sandy responded, "Well, there's no comparison. Mom, please, for once in your life, get what you want."

I not only wanted this house, but also believed it was the house God wanted for me. It was the house I had prayed for. That afternoon I called Janice and submitted my second bid. Four hours later, she called back saying my offer had been accepted and they wanted to close the first week in June.

Closing behind me, key in hand, I unlocked the front door and entered my new home. Still trying to believe it was mine, I wandered into the living room looking at everything with the fresh perspective of ownership. Suddenly, I stopped and stared in wonder at the fireplace in front of me. For the first time I really saw the simple, wood relief, prominently centered on the white face of the mantel frame. It was a Grecian lamp. A lamp? Then a memory flooded back. "You are the light of the world . . ." I strongly sensed that God had a larger vision for me and for this house than I could fathom. It would become a gathering place and be used for ministry. I was home.

That Thanksgiving I hosted the family celebration. The house echoed with laughter and conversation, and the grandchildren were everywhere. Seated at the dining room table, I thought back on all God had done for me that year. With a grateful heart, bursting with adoration for my Father, I gave thanks.

Since that time I have continued to open my home for gatherings of all kinds. And as promised, God has filled my "lamp" so that I could serve His people. To my joy my home has become a place for meetings, ministry, mentoring, and meals for all occasions, and both family and friends have enjoyed staying with me just as the Father had planned. God is fulfilling His promise – I am the light of the world.

I have learned several important lessons from this adventure. When God places restlessness in our spirit it can mean He is about to move in our lives and change is near. This restlessness isn't a reason for fear; it's a call to prayer. In the interim between the petitions of prayer and the full answer, God clarifies our next steps and encourages us in personal ways. No matter the scope of the transition, Jesus is ever sovereign and faithful to bring us into the new.

When I first started praying about a home of my own, I had no idea what kind of house I needed, or how to find one. The house the Lord had chosen for me wasn't even on the market. That's because it wasn't time to move; it was time to prepare to move. It is good to wait patiently on the Lord (Psalm 27:14).

I have also gained insight into praying for my heart's desire. The process begins when we submit our will to the Lord's will and find that His desire has become our desire. This principle remains trustworthy in my life:

Trust in the Lord, and do good;
Dwell in the land, and feed on His faithfulness.
Delight yourself also in the Lord,
And He shall give you the desires of your heart.
Psalm 37:3, 4

part three
stories *of* **light**

LIGHT is illumination,

the opposite of darkness.

The Bible speaks of light

as the symbol of God's presence

and His righteous activity.

Nelson's Illustrated Dictionary[1]

Grace all Sufficient

We are each invited to know the Lord as Teacher. This story is a beloved revelation that He unfolded during my quiet time in August 2006, a full year after moving into my new home. Using a passage of scripture as the foundation, the Holy Spirit showcased His triumphs in my life and specified next steps. I think about this experience often and live in its truth. I will share the revelation as it came to me, precept on precept.

It was just before dawn, my favorite hour of day – especially in summer. Mine is the morning to meet with the Lord, to talk with Him and hear from Him. On this particular day I was enjoying His presence when I felt inclined to read again the first few chapters of the book of Revelation. Eagerly opening my black, leather-bound Bible, I began: *"The Revelation of Jesus Christ, which God gave Him to show His servants what must shortly take place."* In chapter one I read John's vision of Jesus, glorious

Son of Man and Lord of His Church. In chapters two and three I marveled at the correction, instruction, and encouragement Jesus gave to the early church – so relevant to the Church of every generation.

Eventually I reached *Rev. 3:18: "I counsel you to buy from Me gold refined in the fire, that you can be rich; and white garments, that you may be clothed, that the shame of your nakedness may not be revealed; and anoint your eyes with eye salve that you can see."* That gave me pause. This scripture seemed to require action on my part. I thought, "How do I buy gold or white garments? How do I anoint my eyes with salve?"

As I waited before the Lord, He brought to mind a specific Sunday morning back in 1999, just three days after separating from my husband, Rice. After the heartbreak of that week, I was at church in my front-row balcony pew as always. I had remained stoic during the whole service, every raw emotion carefully concealed until the very last hymn. But during the magnificent, pipe-organ prelude of "How Firm a Foundation," the pain surged up and I began to weep. I managed to stifle the sobs, but was powerless to check the blinding tears. My sister-in-law Carol was standing next to me and put her arm around me.

Then something strange and wonderful happened. I will do my best to describe the experience and how it affected me. In that grievously broken moment the Lord began to minister to me. From behind me not far from my right ear, an audible voice began to sing. I glanced at Carol. Yes, she was singing too, but this voice was not hers and it was distinctly separate from the voices of the congregation.

The song was intensely sweet. Indistinct words seemed suspended within the melody of the hymn. The song touched the side of my face very softly, even intimately. Under its duress a transcendent peace flowed to me, then through me, consuming the sting of my grief. Carol seemed unaware of the sound I was hearing. The Singer comforted me alone. *"The Lord your God in your midst, The Mighty One, will save; He will rejoice over you with gladness, He will quiet you with His love, He will rejoice over you with singing" (Zephaniah 3:17).*

In the next days the Holy Spirit continued to emphasize the hymn "How Firm a Foundation." I sensed that the words were important for me to understand, so I searched out an old hymnbook and poured over the powerful charge:

How firm a foundation, you saints of the Lord,
Is laid for your faith in His excellent word!
What more can He say than to you He hath said –
To you, who for refuge to Jesus has fled?

"Fear not, I am with thee, oh, be not dismayed,
For I am your God, and will still give thee aid;
I'll strengthen thee, help thee, and cause thee to stand
Upheld by My gracious, omnipotent hand.

"When through the deep waters I call thee to go
The rivers of sorrow shall not overflow
For I will be with thee, your troubles to bless,
And sanctify thee thy deepest distress.

"When thru fiery trials thy pathway shall lie,
My grace, all-sufficient, shall be thy supply;
The flame shall not harm thee; I only design
Thy dross to consume and thy gold to refine.

"The soul that on Jesus doth lean for repose,
I will not, I will not, desert to his foes;
That soul, though all hell should endeavor to shake
I'll never, no never, no never forsake." [7]

As I meditated on the hymn during those transitional days, the Holy Spirit confirmed that this was His plan for the months and years ahead: "When through the deep waters I call you to go . . . I will be with you." Yes, I would have trials and difficult times, but I had His strong promise. He would be my "refuge, source, and repose." He would be my "firm foundation."

I smiled at the memory. "Lord, I well know how faithful You have been to that promise over the last seven years, indeed over my whole life. You have never, no never forsaken me!"

The sun was rising and my Bible was still open to the third chapter of Revelation. Hadn't one of the verses of the hymn specifically mentioned "gold"? With a bit of detective work I found the journal entry and scanned the hand-copied verses, lingering in verse four.

> "When thru fiery trials thy pathway shall lie,
> My grace, all-sufficient, shall be thy supply;
> The flame shall not harm thee; I only design
> Thy dross to consume and thy gold to refine.

I had questioned the Lord about how to "buy gold" from Him and now I realized that this verse contained His response. Buying gold refined by fire had to do with the process of enduring through trials. So the intense circumstances I had faced at intervals over my lifetime had placed me in a furnace of sorts. I didn't burn up in the midst of them because God's grace had changed the intense pressure and pain into benefit. As I had submitted to the process, the Holy Spirit had purified me. Halleluiah, I had "paid the price" and bought gold from Him each time I had endured by His grace.

Thank you, Lord for gold, but how do I buy *"white garments to cover my shame"?* In answer the Holy Spirit assured me that when I had repented of my sins and received Jesus as my Savior, His own righteousness had covered me (Isaiah 61:10, Rom. 4:7,8). He added to my understanding in Revelation 3:5: *"He who overcomes shall be clothed in white garments and I will not blot out his name from the Book of Life, but I will confess his name before My Father and before His angels."* So I had also kept my garments white by God's grace, the power to overcome. This revelation brought thanksgiving and joy.

Revelation 3:18 continued, *". . . and anoint your eyes with eye salve that you can see."* I was perplexed as I reread these words. Was I blind in an area where I should be seeing? The silence of the Holy Spirit told me I did not have the necessary ointment for my blindness. Lord Jesus, open the eyes of my heart to *all* You want me to see!" The answer to my specific prayer came over the next years in increments as I began searching the scriptures for references to spiritual sight.

In the Old Testament God rebuked Israel for their stubborn refusal to repent for idolatry and disobedience. Though invited to "lift up their eyes," they blatantly refused to see as an act of their will and were alienated from God (Ephesians 4:18). In other places God supernaturally opened the eyes of His servants so they could perceive His glory, a revelation, or supernatural provision (Exodus 33:18 – 23, Isaiah 6:1 – 3, II Kings 6:17). What an exciting prospect!

The writers of the New Testament also described types of blindness and how to apply "salve" so we can see. In one variation we falsely believe that we are rich . . . and have need of nothing when in truth we are wretched, miserable, poor, blind, and naked. When we perceive our true condition, we can humble ourselves, be zealous, and repent (Rev. 3:17). Still another kind of blindness causes us to amplify the sins of others but excuse our own. In this case we must remove the "plank" in our own eye to assist others with the "splinter" in theirs.

Then the Lord began to teach me about a type of spiritual vision that gives us the ability to see our future with God's imagination and wisdom. This adventure changed the course of my life. The Lord revealed that I was living small, looking too much at my feet and not enough at the horizon. It is true that we *"perish for lack of vision" (Proverbs 29:18).*

At this juncture I wrote a vision statement for my life and dared to name the dreams God had ordained for me. Then I actively pursued them in measurable next steps. With practice I began to see more broadly into my potential and in time even stir the latent potential in others. This has been extraordinary for me.

A-heaven-to-earth perspective and dreaming God-sized dreams had never been a part of my life before this revelation. Now I see myself and others as fully equipped to accomplish much in the Kingdom of God. I feel that I am in new beginnings at every front.

Reading, believing, and acting on the truth of God's Word is opening my eyes and giving me the ability to see from His perspective. By all-sufficient grace the Lord is providing gold, white garments, and vision. These gifts add sparkle to my life for His glory.

I have learned to depend on the Holy Spirit as I study His Word. I like to ask Him specific, open-ended questions. Sometimes insight comes in the same moment I ask. At others, I seek a long time then suddenly understanding comes. His guidance is personal and practical. He is powerful, yet gentle, as He helps me apply what He reveals. Opening God's Word is an adventure in relationship.

Lights in My World

My best friend, my mother, was dying. Over the past eight years she had survived several strokes and been moved to a nursing home. Now in August 2003 at age ninety-two, she had suffered a massive stroke and couldn't swallow or speak.

Once, many years before, as we were discussing death, Mother had confided, "I hope I don't die alone." How thankful I was that when her time came to die, I was able to take time off work and never leave her bedside. It was God's gift to her and me.

My siblings, three sisters and two brothers, have always been supportive. During these days we pulled together, doing what we could to comfort Mother and each other. For eight days and nights we talked to her and held her until she passed to Heaven in her sleep. She was buried in the quaint church cemetery in the heart of the community she had loved and served.

The next months were understandably difficult for me. Even though my mother had lived in a nursing home during her last years, a receding shadow of who she had been, I missed who she really was – the hub of our family, a merry companion and newsy conversationalist. I missed her vibrant personality so much.

As we approached our first Thanksgiving without her, we received word that my niece had died unexpectedly. This was shocking news – she was only in her early forties, Susan's age. I was unprepared for how much her death would hurt me. To cope I chose to bury the pain and keep plodding.

To compound my struggle, I contracted the flu in these weeks – the bone-aching kind. And after several weeks the hateful virus digressed into nagging weakness that affected every day, all the time.

Then in the early December, we received word that my aunt, my mother's youngest sister, had suddenly died. She was twenty years younger than mother and the last of Mother's immediate family. Yet again we gathered to ask for the Lord's comfort and surround our cousins with love.

I know that death is a part of life and always with us, but I ached for the loss of three loved ones so close together. To complicate the trauma I couldn't seem to recover from the flu. The weakness shrouded every moment through March, but I dismissed it as part of the grief process. How could I know that the virus would ravage my health for the rest of my life?

Looking back, the Lord comforted me through my family. And although there was no specific word from Him, I knew from experience that He was shepherding me through the valley (Ps. 23). Thankfully, an early spring broke the hold of the grief and flu symptoms. As more months passed, life returned to peaceful normal.

After this season of family loss, a series of personal health issues struck in sequence. In October 2005 I scheduled a routine colonoscopy. Unbeknownst to my doctor or me, Diverticulosis had damaged my colon walls and during the procedure my colon ruptured. Emergency surgery repaired the colon, but I couldn't recover from the surgery. Many days later I was still dependent on IV fluids, a gastric tube to prevent vomiting, and continuous oxygen at fourteen liters per minute. Even when the gastric tube was removed, I was not able to digest food. Why I was not rebounding was a mystery to my doctor. Still I worsened.

Sandy traveled back and forth from her home in Roanoke, Virginia and Susan kept the phone lines buzzing. My church family, and many friends surrounded me with their prayers, fragrant flowers, and visits. My sisters Patricia and Mary traveled from out of town to be with me. When my spirit swung low and I wondered if I would recover, their love sustained me like a kiss from my Father.

On the seventh day at my weakest place, an elder from my church called. Would I like the elders to come, anoint me with oil, and pray over me? Hope rose. "Yes! Please come." Two elders arrived just hours later. They laid hands on me and earnestly prayed for my healing. They specifically asked for wisdom for my physicians. Somehow I knew – I just knew – the Lord had heard their prayer.

Later, at evening rounds my doctor admitted, "I honestly don't know what's wrong, but I have one more trick up my sleeve. I'm prescribing Reglan, a medication for nausea." By the morning of day eight, the Reglan IV medication was underway. I improved immediately. Forty-eight hours later, I was discharged.

It took a while to return to full strength, but in the interim Susan flew in and stayed with me a week and I received an outpouring of love in practical ways. All I could do was praise God.

In September 2006, I scheduled a much-needed hysterectomy. I faced this surgery with some trepidation after the colonoscopy complications. Thankfully the surgery went as planned and I was discharged the following morning. But by evening I was in physical trouble. I couldn't stay awake and my breathing was shallow and labored. At the emergency room, I was told I was in congestive heart failure and transferred to a regional hospital in Greensboro, North Carolina.

Days of testing revealed that the 2003 flu virus had permanently damaged my heart. I was left with an ejection fraction of twenty-five (only twenty-five percent of my heart still functioned). I now had a diagnosis of heart damage, an enlarged heart, and the resulting congestive heart failure. This was distressing news, but there was a blessing too. This explained why the flu had so ravaged my strength, and perhaps why the colon surgery recovery had been so complicated. Once again the Lord loved me through the love of His people. My heart eventually stabilized, and I went back to work, busy and involved in life.

Two years later during a semi-annual cardiology visit, an echocardiogram was ordered to determine if my heart function had improved. The test revealed an ejection fraction of twenty. My doctor gently advised that I put my affairs in order since I was at high risk for sudden death. In paradox I felt well and strong and could do most the activities I had always done. Still, it seemed wise to heed the warning. In the next months, I finalized my will. Then I journeyed on, comforted by the peace of God which surpasses all understanding, that guards my *heart* and mind through Christ Jesus (Philippians 4:7).

One early morning in January 2010, I was hurrying down my front walk to finish packing the car for a busy day of home health visits when my heel slid on a small patch of frozen dew. Up I flew and down I came with a crack into a sitting position on the brick sidewalk. Even in my shock and pain, I knew my hip was fractured.

Within minutes a car stopped. Two women got out and asked if I needed help. One had a cell phone and called 911; the other awakened my adult grandson and granddaughter who were living with me. Seeing the commotion, a neighbor across the street sent her son with a blanket. At these ministrations "The Parable of the Good Samaritan" (Luke 10:25 - 37) flashed through my mind. That morning I was the grateful recipient of the ministry of "good neighbors."

Within thirty minutes of my fall, I was in the emergency room. Surgery was delayed until the next day because of my heart complications. Thank the Lord, with added precautions to protect my heart, this surgery went well, and I was transferred to a rehab center for physical and occupational therapy.

For the next week the pain was so horrendous I was almost unable to function. There were times I didn't have the will to push through to healing. Never the less the persistent staff wheeled me to one of the therapy rooms every day. How thankful I was for them. Slowly, with patient encouragement, I set my will to do the hard work of recovery.

Family and friends visited faithfully. Our church had an interim pastor who had arrived the first of January. Pastor Joe visited several times a week, praying powerful prayers and encouraging me. An added blessing, my granddaughter Rebekah and her six-month-old daughter Emmah were living with me while her husband was deployed to Afghanistan. They came to the nursing home every day, bringing snacks, clean clothes and a good dose of cheerfulness. I was aware again of God's grace abounding towards me through His people.

After many days I began to get past enough of the pain to profit from therapy. I was discharged after three weeks and by the end of May, fully recovered.

My heart seemed stable until the spring of 2011 when I flew to Chicago for my granddaughter Hannah's graduation from Moody Bible Institute. For three days we shopped and explored the downtown area, thoroughly enjoying the sites. I didn't have pain, but a deep tiredness in my chest pressed in. Every few blocks I had to stop and rest. I didn't see this as an emergency since rest put it to rights. But during my next scheduled cardiology appointment in January of 2012, I mentioned these episodes to my doctor, who immediately referred me to a cardiac surgeon for insertion of a pacemaker and defibrillator.

At the appointment the surgeon greeted me with, "I can't decide if you are a cat with nine lives or a tough old bird." I liked him at once. The procedure was scheduled for the end of March. It went well and I was discharged the next day.

Susan flew in from Tulsa to be with me for my first days back home. I didn't feel as strong as I had hoped, but I determined to give myself time to heal.

Sunday was Palm Sunday and I was looking forward to being in church. I was able to dress and go, but I couldn't make it through the service. By Monday I was weaker still. By this time Susan and I were becoming alarmed. She was supposed to fly home Tuesday afternoon, but I was definitely not improving. Tuesday morning came. I felt dreadful and my blood pressure was dropping. I called my doctor and was instructed to come to the emergency room.

I know I have the most fantastic friends on earth and I thank God for giving them to me over and over. I called Pat and Gwen, who graciously drove Susan to the airport, an hour and a half away. At the gate Susan decided she couldn't leave without knowing what was wrong and exchanged her ticket for a Thursday afternoon flight. She rented a car and drove back to the hospital.

In the mean time Mary Ann transported me to the ER where my next nightmare began. After a long night of miserable waiting, I was admitted and eventually transferred to the regional hospital in Greensboro. An ultrasound revealed that one of the electrodes from the newly inserted device had pierced my heart and fluid was building around the area. More surgery was performed to correct the problem.

Complications now became daily events. Easter came and went. My room filled with spring flowers and plants that cheered my days and long nights. Yet I continued to worsen.

It is interesting to feel prayers that are prayed for you. During this time all I could do was lie in bed, sustained by the many prayers lifted to Jesus on my behalf and feebly welcome my family and friends as they visited. In the physical I felt light, almost like I was floating. Mentally, I was cognizant of all my physicians said – and didn't say. But deep inside, my spirit was being held in a firm place of peace and rest. Didn't Jesus say, *"men always ought to pray and not lose heart" (Luke 18:1)?* Suspended in prayer my heart remained in peace.

I was now in day ten of this crisis and still hooked up to wires and tubes. An irritating blood pressure cuff collected readings at regular intervals. At morning rounds my surgeon soberly entered the room and sat down to talk, "The one good thing about coming into your room is your flowers." He was a joy to me and I managed a weak smile. But He had more bad news. The latest echocardiogram had revealed increasing fluid around my heart and the cardiologist who had read the test recommended an invasive procedure to drain the fluid. It had already been scheduled for the next morning.

Now for the first time, I panicked. My mind darted in all directions. I instinctively knew that my body could not survive another procedure. But were my chances of living without it any better? All day and into the night I wrestled with the question. Sometime in the early morning, totally spent, I cried out to the Lover of my Soul, "What do *You* want me to do?" He answered quickly, *"Be still and know that I am God" (Psalm 46:10).*

So I did; I rested in Him. As I submitted, I received the assurance that He was personally directing the decisions of the next hours. The God of the universe had spoken. Nothing else mattered. In the ensuing calm I was as curious as a child to see what He was about to do.

The next morning my cardiologist relayed the new plan. He had talked with my primary cardiologist, and they agreed that I might eventually need the fluid drained from around my heart – but that procedure would not be performed today. They felt it was better to wait and give the injury more time to heal on its own. He announced that I was to be discharged in the afternoon and was scheduled for a repeat echocardiogram Monday morning at 8:00 a.m.

My Bible was open on the bed and he asked, "What are you reading this morning?"

"John," I replied.

"And what did John have to say?"

"That you made the right decision."

He laughed.

My brother James and family came to visit and graciously stayed to take me home. By 5:30 p.m. all the paper work, prescriptions, and instructions were completed, and we were on our way.

My sister Patricia arrived the next morning and stayed for the next week. As instructed, early Monday morning we drove back to the hospital for the prescribed echocardiogram and received the good news. I was improving. With a grateful heart I praised the Lord for His intervention and I thanked Him again for each family member and many friends by name.

As I write this story eighteen months have passed. Last week, I received my third echocardiogram. My ejection fraction is now at fifteen. Despite the apparent decrease in heart function, I feel better than I have felt in years. In the last months I have traveled to an Aglow Conference in California, cruised the inland passage of Alaska, and taken a second cruise up the coast of Maine to Nova Scotia. I intend to spend two weeks this Christmas in Tulsa. I am serving in all the ways I enjoy *with all my heart.*

There have certainly been times over these last ten years when I didn't know if I would live or die. But the uncertainty has taught me to treasure the sanctity and privilege of life. Each day is one more day to love my family and friends "praising my Savior all the day long."

To those who have ministered to me, you are *"children of God"* and have been *"bright lights (stars or beacons shining out clearly) in the [dark] world"* (Philippians 2:14, AMP). I sincerely want you to know how much your encouragement and support have meant to me. Know that my fears are stilled in the knowledge that the Lord is able to keep me in sickness and in health into eternity.

> *The days of our lives are seventy years;*
> *And if by reason of strength they are eighty years,*
> *Yet their boast is only labor and sorrow;*
> *For it is soon cut off, and we fly away . . .*
> *So teach us to number our days,*
> *That we may gain a heart of wisdom.*
> *Psalm 90:10, 12*

I have learned that we were born into families in specific generations and places on the earth for a purpose. As Paul preached in Acts 17, *"He gives to all life, breath, and all things. And He has made from one blood every nation of men to dwell on all the face of the earth, and has determined their preappointed times and the boundaries of their dwellings, so that they should seek the Lord . . ."*

The Body of Christ is a powerful force. We have pastors and church families who shepherd us. Faithful family and friends lift us in difficult times. They are the very hands and feet of Jesus and the light of the world.

Be Aglow and Burning with the Spirit

Seven years after my salvation (1974), I was outwardly flourishing. I had a growing relationship with my daughters, ages eleven and fourteen. I was enjoying nursing and teaching a four-year-old Sunday school class. But in my spirit, I was beginning to long for something undefined. On inspection my spiritual disciplines seemed to be in place: I was spending time daily in Bible study and praying all the time about everything, but I was still unsatisfied. Now I know that the Holy Spirit was creating a desire for more of His presence – so He could fill me.

My response was a fervent personal search for more. I scavenged the local Christian bookstore for new books to feed my spiritual vacuum and devoured them.

During this year the Lord called me to a forty day fast on water alone from Ash Wednesday through Easter. (This was a very unusual invitation from the Lord and by no means for everyone.) How I wish I had kept a journal during those forty days so I could share the insights and joys I received from my Father. I was daily blessed.

The girls and I also attended the spring and fall revival meetings at my home church in Chatham. Stirred by the old hymns and the evangelist's strong sermons in the packed country church, I was somewhat satiated by the end of the week, but within days I would be back to my spiritually famished state.

Here is a spiritual principle I have found true in my life: Times of spiritual hunger are the Holy Spirit's preparation for deeper revelation. Jesus said, *"Blessed are those who hunger and thirst for righteousness for they shall be filled" (Matthew 5:6)*. The Apostle Paul also added perspective, *"But we all, with unveiled face, beholding as in a mirror the glory of the Lord, are being transformed into the same image from glory to glory, just as by the Spirit of the Lord" (I Corinthians 3:18)*. Spiritual growth happens in cycles. Our hunger and thirst are given to birth the next season of our spiritual journey.

And so it was that after more than a year of longing, the Lord used a full Gospel women's movement called *Women's Aglow Fellowship* (Aglow.org) and my matchless *Aglow* friends to mold me into His image from "glory to glory." Here are the highlights of the forty-year plus adventure that followed.

In late August 1975, I took the girls shopping for school supplies and stopped by Hardees for a fast-food dinner. An acquaintance Anna Laura and her daughters were there on the same errand. We joined them and during our conversation she shared that there were several women interested in forming a *Women's Aglow Fellowship* chapter. She went on to say that she and our mutual friend Mary Royster had been meeting to pray for the Holy Spirit to move in Pittsylvania County (the county that encompasses Danville) since the spring of 1973. They believed that *Aglow* was God's answer.

Throughout the fall of 1975 I met with these ladies and several others as the Lord added them. Together, we petitioned the Holy Spirit to raise up an *Aglow* chapter in the centrally located town of Chatham. As we sought the Lord, our minds were opened to greater truths from the scriptures and our hearts were tightly knit.

Anna Laura, who had attended an *Aglow* area retreat, was an enthusiastic leader and brought structure and direction to our prayers. Her spiritual maturity visioned us all. She was one step ahead of me in her walk with the Lord and became a spiritual mentor.

Mary also became one of my inner circle friends. I respected her black and white thinking – I operated in every shade of grey. With her teacher's heart she demonstrated how to dissect and discern – I always leapt in faith. So we balanced and sharpened one another. (If you read the acknowledgements in the front of this book, you will know that she encouraged me to write my story, typed it and completed the first edit.) What a faithful friend in every season.

A short three months later the *Aglow* Virginia Board traveled to Chatham to train and commission us. Anna Laura became president and I accepted the position of vice-president. Mary became our treasurer.

A typical *Aglow* chapter outreach consisted of a catered meal, praise and worship, and a keynote speaker (usually from out of town). Meetings ended with ministry for the needs of the women present led by our speaker and the local board.

We launched our community ministry in February 1976. I'll never forget that much anticipated night. Barbara Ann Chase was our guest speaker. She was a nun when she received the Holy Spirit in all His fullness and was led to leave the convent and establish a ministry for women. She covered many topics, but I was most impacted as she shared her passion for the Sabbath (Exodus 20:8-11). She reminded us that God does not change: it was His idea to rest and keep one day of the week as set apart and holy. She encouraged us to honor Him, laying aside our busyness for a while, and doing the restful things we loved most: gardening, reading, etc. But mostly she encouraged us to sit with Him and allow Him to love us.

She would be surprised to know how carefully I was listening that night. Since that time I have tried to set aside Saturday as a special day to join my heart with the heart of God. In recent years resting in the Lord of the Sabbath has become ever dearer to me.

As enlightening as the speakers were, the most refreshing change was the music – so different from the hymns and hymnbooks that governed worship, as we knew it. Many scriptures were being put to simple choruses. These newly written songs were like wine poured out. No, there was nothing special about their presentation: no beautiful accompaniment, and certainly no cultured voices. Anna Laura just stood at the podium and led a cappella. But spiritual hunger is the best sauce for authentic worship. And the anointing of the Holy Spirit needs no embellishment. As we sang, His sweet, powerful presence taught us to love Him.

It is difficult to describe how transformative this move of the Holy Spirit was for all of us. In those days the gifts of the Spirit were unknown or greatly feared in our area. In *Aglow* mentors demonstrated how to do Spirit-led ministry. Here at last was the missing information I needed to grow. And I was thrilled that my teenage daughters could benefit from these rich spiritual experiences.

We began this adventure as hungry, isolated women, but God had a plan to nourish us as individuals and as a group and in turn bless our community. As He ministered to us, we continued to serve in our local churches out of the overflow.

Each spring brought an *Aglow* retreat sponsored by the Virginia Area Board. What a treasured time, seeing old friends and making new ones, hearing dynamic speakers and learning new praise songs – and I was able to take my girls. The retreats were held in different locations, but the most memorable one was at Eagle Eyrie Conference Center near Lynchburg, Virginia. The keynote speaker was Marilyn Hickey (This was before she was well-known in Christian circles). She spoke that weekend about Nehemiah repairing the broken walls of Jerusalem. During her teaching she compared our personalities to broken down walls filled with holes. How easy it is to see the "holes" (flaws) in the personalities of other people without seeing our own. She asked if we did life with someone who rubbed us the wrong way – we all laughed – and challenged us to embrace them instead avoiding them. In this way God could use them to heal the "holes" in our own personalities.

Again, I was listening carefully with a desire to apply what the Holy Spirit revealed. It so happened that I had a co-worker who frustrated me. As Marilyn spoke I determined to draw near to her – and we ended up friends. Over the years this wisdom has served me well.

In the fall of 1976 Anna Laura and I attended our first *Aglow* National Conference in Seattle, Washington. The conference was a three-day event, but airfare was a better value for a week's stay, so we decided to make a vacation of it. As we made our final approach into Seattle our eyes were pasted to the oval windows in amazement; the whole city appeared to be built into the sides of the mountains.

We had never experienced anything like that conference. Again the worship struck us as wonderful – a glorious magnitude of hand clapping, raised hands, and dancing in the Spirit. We were swept up in the beauty. As the Spirit of God washed over me, I discerned as never before that He loved being loved by His people. Even though I longed to join in, I observed from the sidelines like a wallflower at a ball. I was not yet free enough to worship with abandon.

After the conference ended, we spent three exciting days exploring downtown Seattle. We even splurged for lunch in the restaurant on top of the Space Needle. As it slowly rotated, we enjoyed a spectacular view of the city and Mt. St. Helens. We also visited the church of Dennis Bennett, author of *Nine O'Clock in the Morning*. It was inspiring to be in a church where the move of the Holy Spirit was strong.

One day during our devotion time in the hotel room, I confessed, "I feel as though I pray for the same things over and over without seeing any results." Anna Laura, Bible in hand, turned to the book of James and read with conviction, *"The effective fervent prayer of a righteous man avails much" (James 5:16).* In that moment the Holy Spirit assured me that my prayers did make a difference – even if I wasn't aware of how. Today, I am characterized by persistent prayer.

This conference gave me a heady glimpse of the horizon on many levels. I had not known there was so much more to experience. In Seattle Jesus awakened a desire to worship Him in spirit and in truth.

Then came a transition season for our budding ministry. Anna Laura announced that her family would be moving out of town within the next few months. Tension mounted when Mary and I both felt called by the Holy Spirit to be the new president. We prayed as a board and Mary and I talked, but our relationship was strained. We were still new at hearing God and submitting to one another.

At a monthly outreach during those re-defining months, Mary and I asked the guest speaker to pray with us about this divisive decision. I still remember her response, "What's wrong with your vice-president?" She reminded us that the vice-president was groomed to move into the president's position when it was vacated. That ended the conflict. For the next two years I humbly served as president, praying that the Holy Spirit would mold me into the leader He desired. In the meantime Mary became vice-president, immersing herself in a study of the life of King David, and resting in the confidence that God places each leader into position in His perfect timing. It was a tremendous learning experience for both of us.

I have found that authentic friendship must be tested. Having to face conflict and persevere through to peace forges lasting commitment. In my experience the temporary pain is well worth the fruit of strong, selfless relationships.

The 1977 *Aglow* National Conference was held in Chicago. The National Board encouraged as many local officers as possible to attend, reminding us that if finances were a problem, God could get us there on a "shoestring." Our Chatham board felt the Lord would have us go, but finances were indeed slim. So we prayed for provision. In the end Mary drove her stick shift, economy car – very cozy and skinny on fuel.

"Knowing God" was the conference theme and cry of our hearts. Joy Dawson, well-known author, was the keynote speaker. I still remember with a smile the pale pink dress she wore at one session and as always – trim high heels. She shared from personal experience about having an intimate love relationship with Jesus, emphasizing conversing with Him as a most beloved person. At one point she surprised us by standing on tiptoe, lifting her face, and kissing the air, adding, "He is here. *Love Him!*"

During these three days I more fully realized that Jesus not only indwells me, but saturates my whole world with His reality. This conference was also a turning point in my prayer life: I was inspired to speak to the One I *love*. Sometimes I still stand on tiptoe and kiss the air in the conviction that Jesus, Lover of my Soul, loves me inside out and upside down! *"Where can I flee from Your presence?"* (Psalm 139:7b)

We had only a few hours for sightseeing that year, but we couldn't leave Chicago without taking the elevator to the top of the Sears Tower. I remember how insignificant I felt looking out over the vast, dark city, sprinkled with millions of pinpoints of light. In that moment I better understood that God's light pierces the darkness and that impression seared my soul. *"Indeed, the darkness shall not hide from You . . ."* (Psalm 139:12a)

Then more change – I remarried in June 1978. After a few months, I knew I was to resign as president to focus on my marriage. The Holy Spirit quickened Deuteronomy 24:5 to me, *"When a man has taken a wife, he shall not go out to war or be charged with any business; he shall be free at home one year, and bring happiness to his wife whom he has taken."*

Mary replaced me as president. We were able to laugh at the wisdom of the Holy Spirit in calling us both as president, preparing her to step in as I was called out. God blessed the Chatham Chapter, and two Danville *Aglow* chapters were added, a morning and evening group. They flourished and impacted the city.

By 1984 I was once again serving in *Aglow,* this time as an officer in the Danville Evening Chapter. In the fall of 1986 the *Aglow* National Conference was held in Wisconsin. My daughter

Susan, now married and living in Tulsa, and her first-born, Benjamin, just three months old, met me in Milwaukee. She arrived at our downtown hotel with baby, stroller, a huge suitcase stuffed with "necessities," and a glowing face. Hurray, three whole days together!

The name of the conference was "Prepare the Way of the Lord!" And the uncontested highlight was the presentation of banners at the opening of the first session. Huge banners were processed down the center aisle as Susan and I watched in growing awe from our balcony seat.

We had never seen banners presented as an act of worship. Each was a unique announcement of one of the names of our Great God, richly designed in royal colors. As the women holding them aloft passed below us, the love of God seemed to explode in and around us. With tears washing our faces, we worshiped Him whose name *"is above every name."* I felt as though each participant in the room were ascending a golden highway, preparing the way of the Lord. The unity we experienced was a foretaste of that day when *"at the name of Jesus every knee should bow, of those in heaven, and of those on earth, and of those under the earth, and every tongue should confess that Jesus Christ is Lord, to the glory of God the Father"* (Phil. 2:9b – 11).

The conference ended on a painfully cold day with fine snow in the wind. Susan engulfed the whole stroller with a hearty knitted crib blanket and we dashed to the chocolate factory, whose warm, rich fragrance had beaconed to us each day as we traversed the blocks from our hotel to the conference center. And we couldn't leave Wisconsin without some good Wisconsin cheese. With gifts for everyone crammed under the stroller, we hurried back to the hotel to finish packing and head for the airport. It was heartbreaking to separate at the gate and we sobbed our goodbyes.

In a way my next ten years in Danville *Aglow* were like that sad parting at the Wisconsin airport: packing up the memories and saying goodbye. The Holy Spirit had used Aglow – and many other catalysts – for reviving His Church. To His glory, most women in our area were now enjoying praise and worship, rich teaching, and ministry in their local churches.

Although the board still experienced close fellowship, the outreach meetings were less and less attended. Eventually both Danville chapters disbanded with Chatham following a few years later.

Then in 1999 my marriage collapsed. I felt I was being shaken and pruned. The bare stems that remained seemed lifeless. But Jesus is Lord of winter every bit as much as He is Lord of spring. It was time to heal and rest until due season.

Many years passed. One day in 2006 I received a call from Janice Newcomb, another forever friend, forged in *Aglow*. Over the years I had come to know Janice as a powerful woman of prayer. She was visioned and focused when we needed to "get 'er done," but was queen of spur of the moment fun.

As the new *Aglow* State Prayer Coordinator, she prayed strategically all over the state of Virginia. While interceding for the Danville area, she had strongly sensed that the Holy Spirit wanted to work in our area through *Aglow* once more. Mary, Janice and I met one night for dinner to discuss and pray. Afterward the three of us committed to pray regularly for a fresh move of the Spirit.

But this time the Holy Spirit didn't move large and fast as He had before; He was growing us slow and deep. God was "healing the holes in our personalities" and creating spiritual hunger for a fresh move of the Spirit in our community. We prayed weekly for seven long years, remaining committed "watchmen on the walls" (Ps. 130:6).

In the sixth year, Janice and I attended the *Aglow* Conference in Houston, Texas. Oklahoma was only one state away, so I called Susan and she agreed to meet us.

As I have shared, there is absolutely nothing like an *Aglow* Conference for keeping me connected to the leading edge of the Church and visioning my next steps. This one hosted *Aglow* leaders from one hundred nations. The theme, "The Sound of the Nations," struck us audibly as we entered the hotel lobby where we were immersed in many languages. The conference opened with an Olympic style parade of nations where ladies in their native dress presented their national flags. During worship multicolored praise pennants and streamers swirled in the aisles and front of the auditorium. Oh, the colors – culture – community.

I was further blessed and changed as dynamic keynote speakers Graham Cooke and Johnny Enlow introduced us to "Kingdom perspective." *"Thy Kingdom come, Thy will be done on earth as it is in Heaven" (Matthew 6:10).*

Graham shared a portion of his teaching *The Art of Brilliant Thinking.* Two points particularly broadened my understanding: "We are only challenged by the goodness of God. Every difficulty comes with an upgrade" (*upgrade* - deeper intimacy with God and His abundant provision). Thinking back over my life, I knew this was true. I've had many problems, but God has revealed His goodness in each of them. He has ever been and ever will be my Provision.

Johnny taught from His book, *The Seven Mountain Prophecy: Unveiling the Coming Elijah Revolution.* He charged the Church to influence our nation's seven "mountains" or kingdoms of media, government, education, economy, family, religion, and celebration (arts and entertainment). This teaching inspired Janice's next steps as *Aglow* State Prayer Coordinator. After much research she planned a strategic prayer initiative – to visit the places that represented the birthplace and continuing influence of these seven fields. Since the conference Janice, Mary and I have traveled all over the state to pray for revival on location.

Between sessions we visited The Market Place, a world bazaar of Christian art and crafts in the convention center. Here I found a treasure – a large menorah, handmade from wrought iron, with bee's wax candles.

Best of all Susan and I had an unforgettable three days together. Thankfully our partings are not so heart-rending now. We commit to visit several times a year so separations are not so stretched.

The last conference I attended at the writing of this book was in Ontario California, October 2012. I will share about "Stepping into First Love" in one of the following chapters.

And here we are full circle again . . . Mary, Janice and I, continuing in prayer, have just taken our first steps of faith and have received a charter for an *Aglow* Danville Community Lighthouse. (*Lighthouse* is *Aglow's* new title for a community outreach.) Praise God! We are finally seeing signs of revival in our area.

My *Aglow* friends and I are now in our seventies. We have changed and so has our community. We are in the midst of a *new* work of the Spirit. Yes, it is still based in fervent prayer, authentic worship and deep Bible study. We still invite ladies to come to our outreaches to meet with us, but also feel called to go into their world and meet with them.

In preparation we are doing prayer drives around our city and county, praying for our government, neighborhoods, schools, churches and temples. The Holy Spirit is patiently reaching and we have asked for the privilege of being His conduit of love in fresh ways. He is the great adventure of our lives.

I have learned that spiritual hunger is the preparation for personal revival and in tandem, corporate hunger is the preparation for an outpouring of corporate revival. There is always more of God to be revealed and it is right that we should desire to know Him more and more.

Prayer is the precursor and worship the conduit of the presence of God. I am learning to wait patiently for the Holy Spirit and move with Him as He directs.

I have also learned that deep, long-term relationships are essential for growth into maturity. The Lord weaves friendships into our lives as pleases Him. We influence and complete one another as we persevere together.

It is also valuable to sit at the feet of mentors who are ahead of us in the Kingdom. These spiritual leaders impart wisdom and provide vision for our next steps. In turn we have the privilege of mentoring those who come after us. In this way we all are built up to the glory of God.

Sandra Strange

Many people shall come and say,
"Come, and let us go up to the mountain of the Lord,
To the house of the God of Jacob;
He will teach us His ways,
And we shall walk in His paths."
Isaiah 2:3a

My Song of Songs

Sometimes the Lord inserts a teaser entry into our spiritual glossary so we can begin growing into its simple, profound truth. So it was when He spoke, short and sweet, soon after we moved to Atlanta in 1967. I still remember the moment. Our family had just visited the downtown Cokesbury Bible and Bookstore and was headed back to our car. Unexpectedly, I heard the Holy Spirit whisper, "You are the *Bride*."

"Bride?" I had been gloriously saved only four months earlier and as a spiritual infant, I had never heard that expression. But there on the sidewalk by faith – I heard, I received, I believed. Over the next fifty years He patiently defined this profound truth until I could live in it.

From the early years of my walk with God, I had been drawn to the biblical *Song of Songs,* especially 2:4, *"His banner over me is love."* Though intrigued, I didn't understand it.

It was after Bill's death and our move back to Danville that I spotted *Song of Songs*[8] by Watchman Nee in our local Christian bookstore. Perhaps Watchman Nee, an influential, midcentury Chinese Christian, and favorite author of mine, could shed light on the mysterious meaning of Solomon's love story with the Shulamite maiden. So I bought the book.

Opening my treasure in the family room easy chair was like sailing in the deeps. According to Nee, the biblical *Song of Songs* is a shadow of King Jesus and His Bride. It is a picture of the progression of a child of God as she becomes the Bride of Christ, His Church. I was captivated by this prospect. So over the next years, I dissected and ingested Nee's book. With each reading I recorded the date on the inside cover – a remarkable ten times from December 1976 through April 2011. I never reread that book that I didn't gain fresh insight into the deeper meanings of the biblical *Song of Songs.*

Another intriguing series was *Hinds Feet on High Places*[9] and *Mountain of Spices*[10] by Hannah Hurnard. In these allegories Much Afraid (representing each of us) journeys with the Shepherd (Jesus) to the High Places (a rich relationship with the Lord) and learns to serve in the Valley of Humiliation (the real world). As I identified my life with this journey in subsequent readings, I gained additional wisdom and perspective.

Then in June of 1999 the Lord prompted another bookstore find – *A Kiss A Day*[11] by Jamie Lash. In this book Jamie, a completed Jew, shares her personal experiences as the Bride of Christ in a daily devotional based on the biblical *Song of Songs.* Her book awakened again the desire for intimacy with Jesus. It was her testimony that prompted the faith to ask for "roses for my birthday."

Finally, a life changing revelation of the relationship between Christ and His Church came in October 2012 at the *Aglow* International Conference in Ontario, California, when I stepped into "First Love." I will share this experience in the next chapter.

As you can imagine after all this reading and rereading the biblical *Song of Songs* and my favorite commentaries on the book, I naturally identify my life with that of the Shulamite heroine of the story. Recently, the Holy Spirit revealed that He had orchestrated the events of my life to this end: a fuller revelation of His intimate love relationship for His people.

It has been almost fifty years since the Lord first whispered, "You are the Bride." Now I have taken hold of it. My focus is to reign as the Bride in the Lord's Kingdom, mentoring women in their spiritual growth that they also may know the Lord for themselves.

Below is my personalized narrative of the *Song of Songs.* I would be honored if you would place your name beside mine in this most beautiful of all love stories.

My Love Story *and Yours* from the Song of Songs

Characters:
King Solomon – King Jesus
The Shulamite – the Bride, you and me
Daughters of Jerusalem – the godly friends we influence and who influence us

One early morning good King Jesus is inspecting His fruitful lands with delight and satisfaction when He notices me earnestly at work in the vineyard. He greets me with kindness, even affection. I am surprised that I am worthy of even a glance and wonder how He knows me.

In the ensuing conversation He tells me how happy he is that I have joined those who serve Him. He says that I am beautiful. The stark, strange comment hangs between us, accentuating my obvious blemishes and failures. I cannot meet His honest gaze. How could I know that He has already discerned the true condition of my heart and loved me anyway, that He has paid a price for my presence in His vineyard, that He chose me to serve Him? After a few moments of awkward silence, He smiles and turns with a wave. I watch as his commanding figure disappears among the manicured vines.

But though His physical presence is lost to view, His essence, the effect of His strength and kindness, lingers like perfume. Though I try, I cannot forget Him. I am drawn to Him. Questions about Him dance in my thoughts over the next hours and days. Finally, curiosity overtakes insecurity. If only I could see Him once more – even from afar. But I don't know where to look.

I ask the Daughters of Jerusalem where He grazes His flocks. "Follow the footprints along the footpaths," they encourage. I sense that means that I am to inquire of those who have searched for and found Him before me. I set out and eventually come alongside those I follow.

To my relief they greet me cordially. I learn that in order to continue this holy journey, I must be willing to leave my past behind. After careful consideration, I determine to continue in their company.

As we travel along, they share that when King Jesus "noticed" me, it was His invitation to be in relationship with Him. I realize that I am ready to know and be known by Him. My steps unabashedly quicken.

Eventually – oh joy! – we catch glimpse of Him. Spying my tentative approach, Jesus calls me – by name. I nearly run to where He stands waiting with welcome smile. He is just as I remembered.

We begin to meet together daily. Precept on precept, He teaches me about His Kingdom, describing the particular beauty of each of those who have left their past to follow Him. In turn I share my deepest self. He listens in sovereign silence then speaks truth and wisdom into my experiences. His mercy is like healing salve. His perspective changes mine. He calls me *beloved* and I believe Him. When I am with Him, I am not overwhelmed with challenges and problems. I remain in perfect peace.

To my joy He calls me to serve Him by serving those He loves. I pastor the sick. My joy is nursing them to heath, body and soul. As I minister, I testify to all that King Jesus has done for me and all He stands willing to do for all who follow to Him.

Then our relationship changes. Though I serve in His name and my interests are centered on His affairs, I am wearied by much serving, busy all day. I'm distracted from sitting with Him, my

First Love. My only fellowship is with the daughters of Jerusalem.

To my dismay one morning I realize I have not heard His voice in a long time. The Daughters of Jerusalem ask, "Where is the one you love?" I reply. "He is in His garden." Setting out, I find Him. I repent and we are reconciled. I worship Him, my Beloved, my King. He assures me that He would never leave or forsake me.

Now the King of Glory welcomes me into a deeper commitment. I sit at His feet and gaze at Him. As I study His face, I see the anguish of His cross. I drink from the cup He gives me, losing my will in His. My life is caught up in His. In the intimacy of His love I am satisfied. He has become the lover of my soul.

The next time I see the Daughters of Jerusalem, they are amazed at my beauty. I am filled with the love and light of my Lord – it is His beauty they see. I am aware that I am a reflection of Him.

Almost fifty years ago the Holy Spirit whispered, "You are the Bride." Now I live in that position. He loved me first. Now He is the One I love.

I have learned that Jesus offers each of us His life of love.

* This is the daily walk: reading His Word, worshiping Him, conversing with Him – sharing concerns and listening for His answers.
* This is the primary thing: remaining *in* Him by receiving the love that relentlessly pursues us and in turn loving Him first and best,
* These are the responsibilities: obeying His Word and reflecting all that He is.

We can also learn much from the "Daughter's of Jerusalem." Some of these we know personally and others are the author mentors the Holy Spirit places in our lives. May what *I* write bless others as I have been blessed.

Stepping into First Love

The 2012 *Aglow* National Conference, "Arising to a New Identity" was in full swing. It is extraordinary to be in the midst of hundreds of men and women filled with the Holy Spirit, fervently worshiping God and eagerly sitting at His feet (Luke 10:39). The oneness and purpose in the Body of Christ becomes tangible.

But as we walked the short distance from the hotel to the convention center and took our seats for Friday evening's session, I was more motivated to go to bed and sleep until morning than to revel in the beauty of it all. We had arrived in Ontario, CA on Thursday and the very early morning travel and time change from east coast to west were overriding my excitement. Glancing around I saw I was not the only one in this condition. Many heads were resting on seat backs with stinging eyes gratefully closed.

The keynote speaker for the evening was Graham Cooke. I appreciate Graham's style of speaking – he is able to go from humor to deep teaching without missing a beat. And the topic for the evening session was of great interest to me: the Beloved, the Bride of Christ (the Church of all generations and races). But despite my best effort to be attentive, I was fading in and out, in and out until I heard him say, "First Love." Suddenly, I was alert, straight in my seat, and straining to hear every word.

Graham was emphasizing the position of the Bride in God's affection. To illustrate he presented an impactful skit: Two men representing God the Father and Jesus the Son were called to the platform and stood facing each other, seemingly absorbed in intimate conversation. Graham explained that the space between the Father and the Son is "The Place of First Love," the place designated for His Bride, the Church. There she receives the outrageous love of the Father as it goes through her to the Son and the outrageous love of the Son as it goes through her to the Father. Then he summonsed a third man, representing the Holy Spirit, and directed him to help the "Bride" take her place between the Father and Son. He went straight to Graham's wife, took her by the hand, and guided her into the place reserved for her.

Graham explained that the Bride is so loved in The Place of First Love that she in turn loves others at all times and in all circumstances. As she submits to the Holy Spirit, He continually enables her to abide in a love relationship with God and man. This powerful illustration impacted my imagination to such an extent that it changed my thinking that same moment.

This revelation was the culmination of the Lord's word to me in 1967, "You are the Bride." The Holy Spirit's invitation in the present was clear. So right in my seat, as Graham closed his message, I turned to the Lord in my spirit. As an act of my will by faith, I stepped into the position of First Love as a unique, chosen, beloved Bride. I knew that the Holy Spirit had prompted this action and I had obeyed Him, but I didn't feel different – at first. It was over the next days and months that I realized more fully what I had experienced and my responsibilities and His Bride.

The conference ended late Saturday night. Sunday morning at 4:45 a.m. we were in route to the airport. My friend Phyllis and I had flights together from Ontario to Phoenix departing at 6:00 a.m. From there we each had separate flights on into Virginia via a dizzying network of stops and layovers – a sixteen-hour trip for each of us.

Entering the airport terminal, I went straight to the counter for check in and passed my information to the agent. She studied the computer monitor in growing disbelief, finally exclaiming, "This is the most ridiculous schedule I've ever seen!" Then she proceeded to simplify my itinerary saving me five plane-hopping hours. I called to Phyllis who was in another line, "Our schedules can be changed!" The agent deftly adjusted her flights in a few minutes more, syncing our flights so we could travel together the whole way.

Late in the day we boarded our plane for the final forty-five minute connection into Lynchburg, Virginia. Here my seat assignment amazed me – row one, aisle seat. I had never in all my traveling been close to prestigious row one. Phyllis' assigned seat was mid-coach. As the flight attendant prepared the cabin for takeoff, I noticed an empty seat directly across the aisle from me. Surely it was possible for Phyllis to move forward. But immediately I began to argue with myself. She probably wouldn't appreciate an invitation to change seats after settling in where she was. In the end I did nothing, and the window of opportunity closed. "It's no big deal . . . It's such a short flight," I reasoned. Still my conscience was troubled.

As we landed in Lynchburg the Lord spoke in His still small voice, "You were to have brought Phyllis up to where you are." Stricken, I promptly repented.

As I waited for Phyllis inside the terminal, I pondered the instruction I had just heard. Instinctively I knew the Lord was broadening my understanding using the seat assignment to teach me. I sensed that there was a deeper lesson in this experience and the Lord would unveil it when He was ready. Pausing, I prayed, "Holy Spirit, continue to teach me."

Home at last, weary, but filled to overflowing, I slept undisturbed until 9:00 a.m. – a scandalous hour for me. As I became fully awake, my first thought was, "I feel wonderful." I was very rested, but it was more than that. I sat up trying to figure it out. Suddenly, I realized that I was abiding in the Place of First Love. This reality saturated my spirit, certainly, but also my mind and body. *"The wine goes down smoothly for my beloved, moving gently the lips of sleepers. I am my beloved's and His desire is toward me" (Song of Songs 7:9b -10).*

As promised, the Lord helped me understand more about the "row one" incident in increments over the next months. He desires that each of His "daughters of Jerusalem" come into the place of First Love that we may journey on together in one accord. And I am called to invite them! *"This is my beloved, this is my friend, daughters of Jerusalem" (Song of Songs 5:16).*

This joyful responsibility has increased my ministry and opened new ones: mentoring, outreaches from my home, serving, sharing my faith in small groups, interceding for my family – even writing the book you hold in your hands.

Little did I know that the theme for the Aglow conference, "Awaking to a New Identity," was a prophetic statement for my life. I went in as one person, living in my old pattern, and returned home awakened to a new identity in Christ's Kingdom. The purpose of stepping into the position of First Love is that I may fulfill my call as the Bride of Christ.

I have learned that the heart of our Father longs for us to know Him in a deeper, more intimate way. But our personal joy in the relationship is only the beginning. We are charged to invite others to abide in His love that their *". . . joy may be full" (I John 1:4).*

If the Vision Lingers, Wait for It

Soon after my husband Bill's death in 1972, I began to reflect more fully on God's extraordinary grace in my life. I had just lived through a miraculous season indeed. In the next months a desire to write a book dropped into my heart. I know now that the Holy Spirit was commissioning me to write my testimony for His glory.

After my daughters and I settled into our new lives in Danville, I was finally ready to begin writing. But when I sat with pen and paper, my ideas refused to flow into singing sentences and unified paragraphs. Anything I wrote read like a report – lots of facts, no engaging story.

Once I actually finished ten pages, describing the summer of Bill's and my salvations. But when I began to edit the document, I became overwhelmed and finally set the pages away.

Still the precious stories were always with me, a part of who I was. And in spite of my limitations and discouragement, the dream to write a book simmered in my spirit.

When I separated from my second husband Rice twenty years later, I was driven to journaling for the first time. In these private pages I expressed my despair and dreams unhindered. My broken and disorganized thoughts poured through my pen onto the blank pages – no editing required. I recorded prayers for my estranged husband and the healing of our marriage. I also wrote specific prayers for my family.

As I wrote, Jesus met me in the pages. I was able to release my burdens to Him and found faith to trust Him to work for good in my life. I remembered afresh that I was called for God's purpose (Romans 8:28). He had good plans for me; I had a future and a hope (Jeremiah 29:11). I also found that my "effective fervent prayers availed much" in the lives of those I loved (James 5:16).

I didn't realize it at the time, but journaling was also preparing me to become a writer. Some of my journaled prayers in those years were for the realization of this very book:

December 7, 2000
As another year draws to a conclusion, once again my heart and mind are filled with my book. I want to write the pain, joy, sorrow, peace, hopelessness, forgiveness, unfaithfulness, hope and love of thirty-three years . . . Thank You for my life and Your goodness and thank You most of all for Jesus . . .

September 7, 2002, 4:30 a.m.
Father, I ask to receive the ability to write this book You have placed in my heart. In myself I cannot do it. I will trust You, Lord, to give me the words to write and speak, and to do so with boldness and clarity.

February 22, 2003
I pray, Father, that my life will always please You. I long to reach out to others by writing a book, stories of the wonders You have done in my life. I want to honor You by encouraging others to continue on in *their* difficult times, to persevere and not give up. I want them to know You and believe Jesus is Your Son.

November 18, 2004
. . . King of Kings, today I see myself well, strong, and moving in new directions as a published author and involved in women's ministry. I give to You my plans so You can accomplish them.

January 7, 2005
My Father and my God, I continue to believe You have called me to write a book. I open myself to this call; I want it more than anything. I will continue on. Please, open the way.
I love you, Father. Thank you for Jesus and for sending Your Holy Spirit. Your will be done on earth and in my life as it is in Heaven in Jesus, Amen.

(This was the last written prayer for this book and the only written prayer I ended with *Amen,* which means "So be it.")

Eventually Susan called and asked if I would be willing to tell her the stories of my walk with the Lord and let her write them for me. I was pleased at her willingness to do this. I certainly wanted them to be documented. We worked on this project by phone and in person over several next years.

Christmas 2008 Susan surprised Sandy and me with the finished manuscript called *Beauty For Ashes,* our family story from 1967 – 72. She had mingled her sweetest childhood memories with her dad's and my testimony and included pictures. How the memories flooded back.

More years passed. The first Monday night in October 2012, I attended the Bedford, Virginia *Aglow* Lighthouse meeting with my dear friends, Mary Royster and Janice Newcomb. It was an encouraging meeting of fellowship and worship. We had just returned from the Aglow National Conference in Ontario, California and were still filled to overflowing with "mountain top" love for our Father.

On the way home Mary suddenly asked, "Sandra, when are you going to write your book?"

"Mary! I've tried to write that book for forty years and it hasn't happened."

"You couldn't write it before," she countered. "You had to go to the conference and receive all God did for you there first. Now is the time for you to write your book."

At her words, something exploded inside of me. It was true and I knew it. It was time for me to become a writer.

Tuesday I slept late. Still in rest mode I went out on the front porch to get the newspaper, opened it absently, and scanned the front page. Suddenly a headline caught my attention. The Danville and Pittsylvania County writers' groups were merging. They would be meeting later in the month at Averett University Library, catty-cornered across the street from my home.

I cut the article from the paper and affixed it prominently on the refrigerator door and circled the date on my calendar. I was definitely going to that meeting and that was final. Then I hurried to phone Mary Royster and shared the resonating effect of her words and the unexpected newspaper article. She was as excited as I and reminded me, "I love editing. I will do that for you."

I tried not to think about the humiliation of attending a writers' group with nothing written to share. But a few days prior to the meeting date, inspiration struck. I effortlessly constructed a working outline for my book by naming the many experiences where God's intervention had changed my life, adding a few notes to remind me of some of the details. As I did, I remembered Habakkuk 2:2: *"Write the vision and make it plain on tablets . . ."* Opening my Bible I reread the scripture and as I did, I stepped into my calling to become an author.

On Saturday afternoon, I walked the short distance to Averett Library. It was a perfect fall day. The trees on both sides of West Main Street were maple orange-yellow. I made my timorous way across the broad manicured lawn and entered the building. Climbing the stairs to the second floor, I found the room and I entered short of breath and drowning in anxiety. It was furnished with a comfortable sofa and chairs and I gratefully sank into one of the chairs wondering what writers talked about in their meetings.

There were nine of us in attendance that afternoon. After we introduced ourselves, the leader asked for volunteers to read a portion of their writing. A young woman read a short story she had written for a creative writing class. The man sitting next to me read the introduction to his published book. Then several others read an excerpt of their work. Finally the leader read a chapter from his science fiction novel. There were two men and a woman who looked as lost as I felt. We didn't participate that day, but the meeting was a personal revelation.

I realized for the first time that my dream was within my reach and it was the time to begin. These other authors were writing fiction. I was called to write a story I had lived and knew well. Walking home, I knew with resolute clarity that I had heard, "Come, now is the time." I walked straight into the house, sat down, and started my first chapter.

God is at work in each of our lives. Our unique relationship with Jesus is eternally valuable and beautiful. It is also practical and encouraging. When shared, it is a powerful testimony.

I have learned to wait on God for due season. The grace and anointing to fulfill the vision for our lives comes as God directs. He is able to finish His good work in us in His perfect timing.

For the vision is yet for an appointed time;
But at the end it will speak and it will not lie.
Though it tarries, wait for it;
Because it will surely come,
It will not tarry.
Habakkuk 2:3

Dear Reader,

As a child, when I asked if I could do something adventurous – something that would require money or travel – I was often told, "You can't." And that settled it. There was no money for extra things and no curiosity to pursue anything beyond our experience. As a young woman, I had one goal: to be married and have my children before I was twenty-five. After I accomplished that goal, I never set another. I knew very little about possibilities until Jesus came into my life.

I will be seventy-eight this year. Looking back I could never have asked for or imagined all that God had planned for me (I Corinthians 2:9). And He's not finished with me yet. This last year has been filled with new beginnings as never before. He is the initiator, the Dream Giver and the power for all possibilities.

I pray that my stories have increased your longing to know the Lord for yourself and the courage to live the dreams He has for your life. I am not smarter, or more beautiful, or more spiritual than anyone else. The Lord stands willing to change your life as He has mine. I promise! But more importantly, *He* promises. Your name is written on the palms of His hands. (Jeremiah 29:13, Isaiah 49:16)

Sometimes family and friends ask me to speak into their lives. This book is my response in plain and truthful narrative.

To close, here is a summary of the most practical spiritual principles of my life, those I hope you put to work in your life:

• Seek Jesus. Despite popular theology there is only one way to find God and that is through His Son, Jesus. He is the centerpiece of scripture and the Head of His Church. The Christian life is not a formula; it's a relationship with Jesus. (John 14:6)

- Lean into the Holy Spirit. The third person of the Trinity is a *Person,* God with us. He teaches and guides us, warns and empowers us. He brings His fruit and gifts into our lives. He is grieved by our indifference. In my experience a relationship with the Holy Spirit seems to be a pivotal key to intimacy with God. (John 14:15, 16:5 –14)
- Know that through the death of Jesus, we are the Lord's Beloved. His love for us is beyond our comprehension. *Live* as the Beloved. (Song of Songs 2:16)
- Be a doer of the Word. Go ahead and do what you hear or read. Until you *do* it, the Bible remains inactive in your life. Doing the Word changes you and me first – then it changes our circumstances. Try it. (Matthew 7:24 – 29)
- Live clean. Don't let sin stand in the way of healthy relationships. Be willing to ask forgiveness and give forgiveness as the Holy Spirit directs.
- Praise God in all circumstances – both the hard and easy ones. When things are hard we tend to turn to the Lord for a while then quickly return to worry and self-sufficiency. When things are going well we ride the waves of ease and forget Him. I have found that ongoing praise is a catalyst for victorious living, come what may. (I Thessalonians 5:18)
- Trust in the Lord with all your heart. We can literally throw our cares upon Him because He cares so much. I do this transaction out loud, literally throwing my arms into the air as I name my specific concerns – then I move on in peace. (Proverbs 3:5 – 6, I Peter 5:7, Philippians 4:6 – 7)
- Pray at all times about everything. Pray first. Pray middle. Pray end. (I Thessalonians 5:17)
- Back away from self-centeredness as much as possible. This is a constant battle. I like to remind myself, "You can't have every thing you want, the way you want it, all the time." When I'm frustrated with humility, I sometimes ask, "Well! Who's taking care of me while I take care of the needs of other people?" Then I look back at all God has done for me and I am embarrassed I had to ask. (John 13:14)

Father,

Teach us to number our days,
That we may gain a heart of wisdom.
And have compassion on Your servants.
Oh, satisfy us early with Your mercy,
That we may rejoice and be glad all our days!
Let Your work appear to Your servants,
And Your glory to their children.
Let the beauty of the Lord our God be upon us,
And establish the work of our hands for us;
Yes, establish the work of our hands.

Petitions from the final verses of Psalm 90

End Notes

1 Part I, II, and III Dividers: Herbert Lockyer, *Nelson's Illustrated Bible Dictionary* (Nashville, TN: Thomas Nelson, 1986), s.v. "love," "life," "light."

2 Thomas O. Chisholm, "Living for Jesus" (Public Domain, 1917).

3 Catherine Marshall, *Beyond Ourselves* (Hodder Christian Essential Series, 1962).

4 Nelson's, s.v. "angel."

5 Nelson's, s.v. "humility."

6 Walk to Emmaus, "Prayer to the Holy Spirit" (http://emmaus.upperroom.org).

7 John Rippon, "How Firm a Foundation" (Public Domain, 1787).

8 Watchman Nee, *Song of Songs,* translated by Elizabeth K. Mei and Daniel Smith (Washington, Pennsylvania: Christian Literature Crusade, 1965).

9 Hannah Hurnard, *Hinds Feet on High Places* (Wheaton, IL: Tyndale Publishers, Inc., 1977).

10 Hannah Hurnard, *Mountain of Spices* (Wheaton, IL: Tyndale Publishers, Inc., 1982).

11 Jamie Nash, *Kiss a Day* (Hagerstown, MD: EBED Publications, 1996).